SUPRANATIONAL FOLLY

ETI and the Decentralization of Human Society

Jensine Andresen

CONTENTS

FROM MODERNITY TO POSTMODERNITY

From around 1500 C.E. to its peak in the 1960s, the so-called Modern Period of human history saw the gerrymandering of social-cognitive space into a series of dichotomous categories. From an overarching dichotomy between public and private spheres emanated a series of sub-dichotomies, with the first term corresponding to the public side and the second term corresponding to the private side—secular/religious, history/myth, rational/emotional, authoritarian/free, objective/subjective, and civilized/primitive (with 'primitive' here meaning inchoate and libidinal), etc. (Batstone et al. 1997).

One of the main creations of the Modern Period was the nation-state as a form of social organization. Some people date the inception of the nation-state to the 1648 Treaty of Westphalia, sometimes referred to as the Peace of Westphalia. The Peace of Westphalia ended decades of war and divided political authority in Europe among monarchs, on one hand, and established sovereign states defined territorially, on the other. Borders were not immediately set, however, since monarchs who tried to extend their reach often used ruthless fighters to further their aims in empire building. Nevertheless, after World War II, and especially as territory was redefined in Africa and the Middle East —and then again after the fall of the former Soviet Union—a version of the geopolitical map began to emerge that is similar to what we recognize today (McFate 2014).

In addition to the creation of the nation-state, another key element of the Modern Period was the rise of so-called Enlightenment thinking, which catalyzed the American, French, and Russian Revolutions. The rise of the free market economy, mechanization via mass production somewhat typified by Fordism, and mass education also arose during the Modern era. As did mass democracy, secularization, humanism, classical physics following the Newtonian paradigm, scientific materialism, modern medicine, and vaccination (Jencks 1996).

As time went on, the Modern Period gave way to the Postmodern Period, which began to gain traction in the 1960s and 1970s and continues in certain forms today. Postmodernity's two most prominent features are privatization and globalization. Privatization involves taking companies that previously were held commonly by the public and selling them off to monopolistic, private interests that then can control the market values for the underlying resources. Ideologically, privatization is an homage to the theory of laissez-faire capitalism, which favors so-called free market capitalism with no government intervention. Closely related to privatization is globalization, which itself has two key features, namely the globalization of finance capital and the deindustrialization of economics. Both of the latter two features also function as the main economic and industrial backdrops of postmodernism. Both globalization of finance capital and the deindustrialization of economics support the consolidation of money, power, and control in the hands of a relatively few, socioeconomically elite members of society. Overall, both the forces of privatization and the forces of globalization contribute to the formation of a socioeconomic 'elite' while socioeconomically marginalizing other members of society (Batstone et al. 1997).

From the utilitarian perspective of globalized finance capital, first world, industrialized nations are obsolete. The economy is autonomous, without allegiance to any one nation, community, or laws. Hyper-capitalism—which is the complete rule of automatized and self-determining capital—has become the norm. In addition, consumption rather than production has become the primary mode of integration in the expanded, global market, and workers have become providers of services instead of mediating capitalism and labor movements, as they did in the past (Batstone et al. 1997).

One tragic aspect of postmodernity is the way it supports, if not elevates, rabid individualism and greed. People fight less over principles and more for financial gain. War profiteering is one example of immoral greed, with defense contractors, weapons manufacturers, and private financiers using manipulation to pit one side against the other until violent conflict breaks out. Then, conflict persists because it is profitable, as is rebuilding after conflict. Two of the greatest sources of making money today are war and reconstruction after war, which create numerous financial opportunities for companies such as BlackRock and many others (Smith 2022; Dixit 2023; Masters 2023). At some point, human beings need to realize that in order to survive as a species, we must dismantle our militaries and cease weapons manufacturing across the globe. It is the only way to survive while also restoring humankind's moral integrity (Andresen 2023b; 2023c).

Today, the once dominant nation-state mode of organizing society is on the wane as power and control are being consolidated into two main blocs of nations, NATO and BRICS. At the same time, we still have three global superpowers, i.e., the U.S., China, and Russia, other functioning nation-states, numerous fragile states, and an increasing group of failed states (WPR 2022). What we need to realize is a true multipolar world, with many functioning nation-states that work cooperatively with one another laterally, instead of by means of the hierarchy of blocs.

As globalized finance capital renders many first world, industrialized nations obsolete, however, we are seeing an increase in chaos globally, followed by an increase in the consolidation of power and authority that claims it will 'resolve' that chaos. For at least the past three hundred years, as nation-states become vulnerable and sometimes fail, supranational interests have swooped in to buy and sometimes take their resources. Supranationals buy these resources of fragmenting countries at rock bottom prices. This is one of multiple reasons why as the organizational form of the nation-state collapses, the rich get richer while the poor get poorer.

Superpower fragmentation is seen today in the U.S., China, and Russia. In addition, smaller groupings of countries such as the European Union (EU) also are fragmenting. In the case of the EU, this fragmentation gained momentum with Brexit. Now, civil society is fragmenting across much of Europe as fierce internal debates on immigration rage within many countries, with violence breaking out in France in protest of racist policing (Strauss 2023).

Meanwhile, as fragmentation is occurring within individual countries—nation-states as a group are consolidating into two large blocs. On one side is the U.S. and its NATO allies, together with Sweden (which is in the ratification process), Ukraine (which has applied to NATO), and Bosnia and Herzegovina and Georgia (which have notified NATO formally of their wish to join the Alliance). On the other side are the BRICS nations—Brazil, Russia, India, China, and South Africa—and those countries that aspire to join BRICS, such as Algeria, Argentina, Bangladesh, Burundi, Comoros, Cuba, Democratic Republic of Congo, Egypt, Gabon, Guinea-Bissau, Indonesia, Iran, Kazakhstan, Mexico, Nigeria, Saudi Arabia, the United Arab Emirates (UAE), and Uruguay (Sguazzin 2023; MEM 2023; MFARI 2023; Devonshire-Ellis 2022). The U.S. has tried to coax India out of BRICS, so far to no avail (Kaushik 2023).

The conditions supporting further consolidation of the world into two blocs has intensified even more since Russia's recent invasion of Ukraine in February 2022. But the problem with consolidation—and why we should work toward multipolarity instead—is that consolidation makes it even easier for supranational individuals, entities, and networks to concentrate control within human society, since consolidation means there are fewer organizations and/or networks to control. Currently, with tension between NATO and the BRICS so high, it becomes clear that real, substantive (i.e., ontological) change in how we think as human beings is necessary to overcome this standoff (Andresen 2023b).

The 'two bloc' landscape is replacing what previously was referred to as the "Game of Threes," or the "New Great Game." In the Game of Threes, the world was organized according to a tripolar model with the U.S., China, and Russia, and their respective spheres of influence in competition geographically, economically, and intellectually. Russia and China shared the goal of reducing Western and particularly U.S. influence worldwide, while the U.S. was doing a very good job of sabotaging itself by permitting partisan politics to run amok (Bittner 2018). Even when the three major world powers were involved in the so-called New Great Game, however, the dynamics were substantively different than earlier attempts of the Capitalist West and the Communist East to contain one another during the Cold War (NYT 1996; Kleveman 2004).

THE SUPRANATIONALS
AND THE ULTRARICH

During the postmodern period, money—both access to it, and, also, the ability to manipulate it by controlling the money supply—has proven key to the rise of the elite and their formation of a worldwide, supranational network. The supranationals, as I call them, have *almost unlimited access to finance capital* and exert considerable control regarding *the expansion and contraction of the money supply*. By controlling the volume of money, supranationals control industry, commerce, energy, logistics, and almost everything else on which other members of society depend. As the link between finance capital and the nation-state has been severed almost entirely by the unfolding of globalization from the 1960s to the present—and as technological innovations have made finance capital more mobile—the supranationals have gained control over even more.

Supranationals, many of whom engage in financial and other modes of criminality, often operate in networks that sometimes scapegoat one of their own to hide a network's very existence. A prime example of this is Jeffrey Epstein, whose enormous network of ties has begun to be revealed. Still, because the media focuses attention almost exclusively on Epstein's sexual deviance and criminal behavior, many people do not realize how large his network of associates really was, and the extent to which it was involved in financial and other forms of criminality (Bensaid 2019; Webb 2022). Of course, not all supranationals are overtly criminal, yet many nevertheless are quite skilled at using the legal system—together with private, corporate, and even non-profit mechanisms such as foundations—to concentrate power and control in human society. There seems to be virtually no 'trickle down' effect—instead, everything is percolating up, and the concentration of wealth is increasing by the minute.

Supranationals seek control over resources such as coal, oil, natural gas, land, real estate, etc. For this purpose, they often target countries in Africa and elsewhere that are rich in natural resources in order to create monopolistic control of mining rights for uranium, lithium, tantalum, zinc, Jadeite, diamonds, etc. These same interests control natural resources such as water, and raw materials such as steel, corn, grain, lumber, etc. Water is particularly precious, and depending upon where one lives in the world, water can be even more valuable than oil.

Supranationals also control vast swaths of the logistics and supply lines around the world, such as shipping, trucking, rail, etc.; pharmaceuticals; insurance; satellites; travel and tourism; and other industrial technologies such as steel production; etc. Finally, supranationals exert tremendous control over the media by buying up newspapers, media networks, and social media platforms outright. Also, by launching various 'alternative' media platforms that they try to make look 'independent' when in reality they are nothing more than mouthpieces trumpeting the supranationals' own agendas. In the U.S., for example, the ability of official entities within the USG to control the narrative in mainstream media—itself a problematic reality—is waning as supranational-controlled media outlets are gaining traction. What we have yet to realize is a truly independent press.

Supranationals come from every major country in the world—Americans, Brits, Western Europeans, Russians, Chinese, and many other nationalities are represented in the supranational class. Post-Soviet statists, oligarchs, and kleptocrats often function as supranationals—but so do Western international bankers. While some supranationals may trace their family lineages back to the monarchical class, what really holds this group together is a shared sense that they are entitled to control others. Many supranationals are international bankers themselves, while others work closely with transnational financiers and other corporate heads. Regardless, supranationals promote globalization, since their own business interests transcend national boundaries. This globalist agenda often benefits the supranationals while weakening the nation-state. Whereas individual countries offer citizens some social assistance, the supranationals offer none. The result is the unimaginably unjust and socioeconomically stratified global society that we have now. Meanwhile, while the supranationals concentrate wealth and power in the hands of a few and amass personal fortunes that eclipse the resources available to others, they often appear completely oblivious to the horrific direct and indirect violence they are perpetrating on billions of people who are less socioeconomically fortunate.

Because of the dynamics described above, traditional nation-states face tremendous competition from two directions. At one level, nation-states compete with one another, e.g., the competition between the U.S. and China. But all nation-states also compete with the supranationals. As both types of competition increase, surveillance of citizens also is increasing across the board.

The entire concept of competition is based on the scarcity mindset, namely the idea that resources are scarce, and that the group with the greatest control over the distribution of resources and money 'wins.' Although this mentality has been part of human society for centuries, it is atavistic now that the most serious challenges facing humankind—climate change, pandemics, mass migrations of human beings and other species, etc.—are global in nature. Competing over resources will not help us resolve pressing global issues. Instead, we must realize that reality is a whole, matter and consciousness are inseparable, and everything that exists does so by means of participation (Andresen 2023b).

In addition to the supranationals, another group of people who have concentrated money and power over the past few decades are the ultrarich. The ultrarich are multibillionaires such as Elon Musk, Jeff Bezos, Bill Gates, Larry Ellison, etc. Some ultrarich individuals have amassed fortunes greater than the GDP of many nations combined—which, obviously, is deeply problematic from the perspective of social justice.

However, the supranationals and the ultrarich are not precisely the same in many cases, since another layer of stratification in human society falls along the 'old money' versus 'new money' divide. Given enough time, however, the ultrarich and their descendants sometimes become supranationals, or they break into the supranational class in other ways. Bill Gates in a case in point, as someone who has moved from the category of 'ultrarich' to 'supranational' status now that his agenda is more intertwined with that of the global elite.

Although this is a vast overgeneralization, traditionally the ultrarich have been more aligned with nation-states as compared to supranationals, since the ultrarich have depended on nation-states to provide them with opportunities to make money. This trend has begun to change, however, as ultrarich individuals have started buying up more media interests. For example, when Musk purchased Twitter, he obtained more autonomy from the nation-state and more leverage to influence political decision-making.

At least four ultrarich individuals—Musk, Bezos, Richard Branson, and Robert Bigelow—have made significant investments in space. Moving quickly without the need to negotiate Byzantine government bureaucracies, Musk and Bezos both developed private launch capabilities, and they currently compete with one another for military launch contracts. As such ultrarich individuals stake claims on space, their personal opinions on the future of humankind—right or wrong—already are shaping the direction of events. For example, Musk wants to colonize Mars, and Bezos wants to create O'Neill colonies. It should not be left in the hands of the ultrarich to decide for all humankind how space exploration should look. Clearly, a much more inclusive conversation is merited. However, as I describe elsewhere (Andresen 2023c), the inadequacy of international space law means that a relatively few individuals with sufficient wealth are making decisions regarding space on behalf of the entire species. How humankind ventures into space should elicit a broad discussion at a global level, and it should not be left in the hands of the elite.

From the perspective of competition, the greatest competitors of the supranationals are not the ultrarich—who in many cases aspire to become supranationals themselves one day—rather, they are nation-states. Nation-states have vast economic clout derived from taxation, which funds the formal militaries and intelligence/covert operation apparatuses of the world. The institutions of the nation-state around the world also employ millions of people, who are beholden to the state for their livelihoods.

Since the nation-state is the only entity with enough money to resist the global elite from taking over human society entirely, the nation-state is a natural foe of the supranationals. Yet the supranationals themselves often benefit from nation-states and their taxpaying citizens. Supranationals tap into nation-states financially by issuing loans and other forms of credit to finance wars, while they meanwhile collect interest and fees. Supranationals also often manipulate nation-states into appropriating funding to support the preferred projects of the elite—for example by contributing to the campaigns of people whom they can pressure—regardless of whether these projects benefit others. In addition, supranationals and governments share the desire to consolidate control—which means they sometimes team up to support projects that increase surveillance. Both groups rhetorically claim that to deliver security, they must 'collect data' on citizens and restrict citizens' freedoms. Of course this is false, because over the long run, it does nothing but further the distrust of the citizenry in the apparatus of the state.

A hybrid organizational form between nation-states on one side, and either supranationals or more often the ultrarich on the other, also has developed in recent years. As described elsewhere (Andresen 2023c), this is expanding the world of private contractors, especially Private Military Contractors (PMCs) and Private Military Firms (PMFs). PMCs/PMFs make inordinate sums of money from contracts paid for by the state, which means that ultimately, it is taxpayers who are footing the bill.

The configuration of actors described above—nation-states, supranationals, and the ultrarich—is the same whether one lives in a liberal democracy or in an authoritarian state. The only difference is that in liberal democracies, elected officials stand between the supranationals and the state, while in totalitarian and authoritarian regimes, dictators and their subordinates are in that position. In years past, both elected and dictatorial leaders tended to be more aligned with the nation-state than with supranationals, though this is changing in many areas of the world. Now, the supranationals are gaining more sway, ironically especially in the U.S. where they ally themselves with members of the U.S. Congress.

The U.S. is particularly vulnerable to the influence of the supranationals because of the dynamics of the American electoral system. Instead of sanely instituting a direct democracy, the U.S. still relies on atavistic 'representative' democracy. To 'represent' a constituency, people must 'run' for office. One of many problems is that elections in the U.S. are exorbitantly expensive (Andresen 2023b, 245-46). Unless someone is independently wealthy, running for office depends upon one receiving campaign donations. This makes elected officials in the U.S. very vulnerable to the influence of the supranationals, who often make large campaign donations. Many elected officials in the U.S. end up doing the bidding of supranationals rather than acting in the best interests of their constituents. Unsurprisingly, campaign finance reform does not occur in the U.S., since Congress would need to enact such laws, which would subvert the interests of their supranational donors. This simply does not happen, for obvious reasons.

The concentration of money and wealth is increasing (Alcorn 2020; see also Desjardins 2020). However even a decade ago, the top 1% of Americans took in nearly 25% of the nation's income every year. Furthermore, the top 1% of Americans control 40% of the wealth. Wealthy people make the campaign donations necessary to keep this unjust system in place and to ensure that tax policies in the U.S. favor the rich. By lowering tax rates on capital gains—which is how the rich receive a large portion of their income—the wealthiest Americans have close to a free ride. As economist Joseph Stiglitz (2011) comments, during the savings-and-loan scandal of the 1980s, banker Charles Keating was asked by a congressional committee whether the $1.5 million he had spread out to a few key elected officials could buy influence. He replied, "I certainly hope so."

Supranationals also dominate many international organizations, such as international non-governmental organizations (INGOs). Interestingly, INGOs have no legal status, even though they are able to obtain consultative status with the Economic and Social Council (ECOSOC) of the United Nations (UN) —and, tellingly, such status often is reserved for them (UN n.d.).

Both nation-states and supranationals have their natural advantages as they compete against one another. Nation-states have access to classified information amassed by the high-tech sensor systems operated by their military and IC communities, as I describe elsewhere (Andresen 2023c). Although PMCs/PMFs and other private contractors in the defense and IC industries often do have some access to classified information on weapons development and sensitive military and intelligence gathering technologies—which is the reason people refer to a military-industrial complex (MIC) (Freeman and Hartung 2023)—classified information can be more difficult for most supranationals to access because many of these individuals does not want to come out of the shadows long enough to go through the clearance process.

With respect to classified information in particular, it is obvious that nation-states also compete directly with one another. For example, the U.S. and its NATO allies are targets of very aggressive espionage efforts by China, Russia, and other countries to obtain access to classified information on weapons and other sensitive topics. This sometimes even involves perceived allies such as Israel passing U.S. classified information to China (Military.com 2013). But the U.S. also aggressively targets other countries in its own pursuit of their classified information and technologies. So, espionage occurs in all directions.

HUMAN AGENDAS TO CONTROL OTHER HUMAN BEINGS

The desire of some human beings to control others is nothing new. This mindset manifests in many forms of thinking, such as proto-fascist, fascist, authoritarian, and totalitarian frames of mind.

People who want to control others often use conflicting ideologies to pit one group against another according to the classic strategy of 'divide and conquer.' Ideologies are powerful because human beings often are swayed by narratives and stories—which is why supranational forces are trying so hard to control the narratives regarding topics in which they are interested. By using conflictual narratives to polarize human society, supranationals manipulate people into vilifying, persecuting, and killing one another, which creates the conditions whereby the elite further consolidate their own control.

To realize their misguided objective of a unipolar, supranational-controlled world, the supranationals often pit one nation-state against the other in a choreographed repetition compulsion of violent conflict, with no single nation-state ever achieving complete geopolitical dominance. Indeed, a true, nation-state hegemon would create a real competitor to the supranationals—so the supranationals step in before a real decisive victory is won by any single nation and compel the warring sides to compromise. Meanwhile, international bankers have profited from both sides of the conflict, and companies such as BlackRock profit from the reconstruction.

Opposing a thesis to its ideological antithesis creates conflict that weakens natural, cooperative bonds between human beings. But when society is divided, the supranational elite become even more powerful—especially when they control both sides of the conflict. High financial powers have used this strategy to great personal and corporate effectiveness over the past few hundred years. Ruling the world by proxy, the poor fight and die to further the agendas of the elite, while the elite themselves remain in the background, financing and profiting from both sides of the fray. In this type of scenario, politicians are nothing more than temporary figureheads to be replaced, one after another, while the elite pull the strings.

Human beings are easily manipulated by means of ideology, which the elites in power know. Supranationals therefore are masters at creating polarized narratives in order to drive people apart. One apparent thesis and antithesis after another have been used to incite conflict—e.g., the communist thesis of Karl Marx was opposed by Karl Ritter's antithesis; fascism has been opposed to Marxism, Nazism, anarchism, democracy, and liberalism. In turn, Marxism has been opposed to many things, most notably capitalism. Polarizing ideologies involving religious themes also are common, such as atheism vs. religiosity; atheism vs. theology; atheism vs. Christianity; etc. The history of humankind is one in which otherwise good people are co-opted into harming and killing one another by appeals to misplaced patriotism, which rides on the backs of polarized ideologies. When individuals are not so easily persuaded, they can be paid exorbitant amounts of money to function as mercenaries or simply be conscripted.

Two historical examples show how effective the divide and conquer strategy has been in helping the supranationals gain control over large parts of society. First, in 1945, as scientists were racing to develop the atomic bomb, the ideological conflict surrounding the war distracted people from the actions of supranationals, who were busy increasing their financial control over human society. Second, when the United States was forming —to the alarm of every monarchy on the globe—the high financial powers of Europe divided the U.S. into North and South and prodded the two sides into conflict to try to prevent the U.S. from achieving economic and financial independence. This strategy enabled the high financial powers of Europe to retain their financial domination of the world.

If history can teach us anything, it is that we should follow our principles rather than becoming caught up in ideological conflicts that benefit the elite. Every individual should have an actual opportunity to achieve financial independence from monarchical and/or supranational control.

NATION-STATES AND SUPRANATIONALS BOTH PUSH FOR UNIPOLARITY

Nation-states and the supranationals have one goal in common—both are pushing for a unipolar world—though of course it is not the *same* unipolar world. Each wants a world that it controls.

Many nation-states, including unfortunately the U.S., are continuing to seek hegemony. In 1997, the Project for the New American Century (PNAC), which was supported by Donald Rumsfeld, Dick Cheney, and Paul Wolfowitz, articulated a blueprint for U.S. hegemony. Neoconservatives such as Victoria Nuland and others who are hellbent on U.S. hegemony still hold positions of considerable power in the national security establishment of the U.S. Demonstrating that the U.S. hegemonic aspirations are not limited to one political party, Nuland has served in important positions in the U.S. under both Republicans and Democrats. Nuland used to be Cheney's security advisor before becoming the U.S. ambassador to NATO, where she pushed for NATO enlargement. Subsequently she then became Hilary Clinton's spokesperson, then Assistant Secretary of State for European Affairs, and now Undersecretary of State. Regardless of what party was in power, the shared hegemonic strategy of both neoconservatives and liberals has remained the same (Neutrality Studies 2023).

Supranationals share with nation-states the goal of global hegemony, though the supranationals are pushing toward a unipolar 'one world government' that they control economically by means of a global central bank. In contrast, nation-states are seeking military and intelligence hegemony rather than strictly financial power. Historically, supranational elite bankers have controlled the money supply using the international system of central banks, which has created an invisible government of the monetary power as opposed to governance in the traditional sense. Establishing a central bank is a central element of controlling a country, since whoever controls the volume of money controls industry and commerce. This is the real globalist objective, namely to combine the supranational sovereignty of international bankers with input from a few intellectual elite in order to try to supplant the auto-determination of individual nation-states (KI 2023).

Given that a small network of interconnected central banks currently are coordinated from a central hub, namely the Bank for International Settlements (BIS), elite financiers have almost achieved their goal of unitary, economic power. Created at the Hague Conference in 1930, BIS is the oldest international financial institution (BIS n.d.-b). Headquartered in Basel, Switzerland, it is near—or at—the pinnacle of the societal control hierarchy for the entire world. Owned by sixty-three member central banks, BIS has representative offices in Hong Kong and Mexico City. Functionally, BIS is the central banks' bank. Its member central banks represent countries around the world that together account for approximately 95% of world GDP (BIS 2022). BIS went from 33 shareholding central bank members in 1995 to 60 in 2013, which reflects BIS' push for globalization and its strategy of breaking out beyond its European core. In March 2022, the BIS suspended the Bank of Russia's membership, though prior to that, the Bank of Russia was part of the network.

Given BIS' clout on the world stage, one would think that mainstream media would cover BIS' activities every day. Yet the mainstream media almost never mentions BIS, and many people have never even heard of it. Nevertheless, individuals such as Jerome H. Powell from Washington, D.C. and Christine Lagarde from Frankfurt am Main sit on BIS' eighteen-member Board of

Directors, which is chaired by François Villeroy de Galhau from Paris (BIS n.d.-a). Because of its opaqueness, however, BIS has begun to come under well-deserved scrutiny in recent years (LeBor 2013; Fields 2013).

In partnership with the central banks of Israel, Sweden, and Norway, BIS currently is promoting a project called the Icebreaker, "to observe the technical feasibility and prospective efficiency of cross-border and cross-currency transactions between experimental retail CBDC [central bank digital currencies] systems" (Nicenko 2023). This comes shortly after BIS set stultifying limits on bank exposure to crypto markets (PYMNTS 2022) in a not-so-subtle effort to retain its dominant position in international banking and financial markets.

Consolidation of control in the global banking sector is increasing rapidly. For example, Europe's wealthiest families have joined together to take the Paris-listed investment bank Rothschild & Co private. The largest shareholder of Rothschild & Co is Concordia (Campden 2023). Rothschild & Co Concordia is a French simplified joint-stock company, all the members of which are members of the Rothschild family (MarketScreener 2023). Also participating alongside the Rothschild family as long-term stakeholders in this take-private is the Dassault family. Its Groupe Industriel Marcel Dassault controls interests across media, software, aviation, etc. Another participant is Giammaria Giuliani, an Italian multi-generation family member and health entrepreneur. Both the Dassault family and Giuliani already were investors in Rothschild & Co. Additional participants in the venture are Etablissement Peugeot Freres, the holding company of the car firm-owning Peugeot family; Mousse Partners, family office for the Chanel-owning Wertheimer brothers; and Hannah Rothschild, the daughter of Jacob Rothschild who in the late 2010s broke with the British branch of the Rothschild family to pursue his own interests. The Rothschild family is of the view that all these long-term investors have a relationship of trust with the family (Campden 2023). What all clearly have in common is that they are supranational.

DE-INDIVIDUALIZED PERSONS SEEK POWER AND CONTROL

Whether it be horizontal conflict between two groups with relatively equal power, or vertical conflict between a group with significant power and one without it, conflict usually is about control. Supranationals like control.

Control dynamics are based on an exaggerated sense of distance, which is inaccurate ontologically from the perspective of the whole described by Bohm. In the whole, everything participates in everything else (Bohm 1990, 275). In contrast, dynamics involving the pursuit of control are based erroneously on the misinformation that a system can be broken down into independently existing parts.

Psychodynamically, what Carl G. Jung refers to as "de-individualized persons" are most susceptible to becoming enmeshed in control dynamics, either as the person attempting to control or as the person(s) being controlled. Jung describes de-individualized persons as follows:

> Naturally, society has an indisputable right to protect itself against arrant subjectivisms, but, in so far as society itself is composed of de-individualized persons, it is completely at the mercy of ruthless individualists. Let it band together into groups and organizations as much as it likes—it is just this banding together and the resultant extinction of the individual personality that makes it succumb so readily to a dictator. A million zeros joined together do not, unfortunately, add up to one. Ultimately everything depends on the quality of the individual,

> but the fatally shortsighted habit of our age is to think only in terms of large numbers and mass organizations, though one would think that the world had seen more than enough of what a well-disciplined mob can do in the hands of a single madman. Unfortunately, this realization does not seem to have penetrated very far—and our blindness in this respect is very dangerous. People go on blithely organizing and believing in the sovereign remedy of mass actions, without the least consciousness of the fact that the most powerful organizations can be maintained only by the greatest ruthlessness of their leaders and the cheapest of slogans (Jung 2006 <1957, 1958>, 55-56).

De-individualized persons often are willing to inflict direct and indirect violence in order to try to consolidate money, power, and control without considering the wellbeing of the whole. Because they perceive things egocentrically, they are prone to negative projection and the creation of an artificial distance between oneself, understood as one's ego, and the perceived 'other.' This also can occur in a geopolitical context, when one country describes another as an 'evil other.' This often is used by the former as a pretext to try to excuse the aggressive and violent actions against the latter.

In contrast, understanding that existence is a whole naturally dissipates the tendency toward projection. Because we all participate in a whole, our participation must be based on moral integrity and developing one's full potential for the good. Looking within and adjusting one's own behavior has nothing to do with trying to control others.

In the grand scheme, accumulating material possessions means nothing, since genuine freedom arises from an integrated psyche. In contrast, the impetus to control others arises from a fragmented psyche in which aggressively defensive psychological structures function as offshoots from one's authentic inner self. Furthermore, trying to control the external environment in order to try to create a sense of inner order and assuage inner vulnerability is doomed to fail. It depends on psychological compartmentalization, when what one really needs is cognitive integration.

Many people with fragmented psyches—"de-individualized persons," as Jung calls them—have been born into roles that they did not create themselves. They may be replaying earlier psychological scripts, into which they and members of their families have been socialized over generations in elitist family units and, also, often in elite boarding schools. Such individuals often hold their scripts at such a deep, unconscious level that they are unaware the scripts were written by others. Even though such individuals are elite socioeconomically, they have been robbed of their chances to explore the fullness of reality around them.

While we can be empathetic regarding the inner wounding and psychotic impulses that cause people to become despots in the first place, we should not turn a blind eye to the social injustice for which such "de-individualized persons" are responsible. Tremendous suffering and inequality arise from the consolidation of control over Earth's resources and the global money supply, and when power and wealth continue to be concentrated in the hands of fewer and fewer individuals, family networks, and entities.

Of course, the impulse to control reaches a zenith of sorts when people embody the intention to dominate Earth itself. A domination mindset is anathema to responsible ecological conduct, since 'resources' are extracted and large areas of land are laid bare. Tragically, ecological devastation tends to hurt vulnerable people more than the wealthy, who often can insulate themselves against its impact. When a socioecological system is severely out of balance, however, chaos can erupt suddenly and widely, which impacts everyone, the rich included. Meanwhile, ecological devastation often has horrific consequences for the poor, who are killed when climate change contributes to all manner of chaos, including violent storms and rising seas.

Ultimately, the entire concept of the 'environment' is much larger than an Earth-centric context. The real environment is the whole, which is why genuine human action must be oriented toward contributing constructively to the whole. If we can renew the environment on Earth and become stewards of a peaceful mode of existence, we naturally will devote the resources necessary to plant trees and green the deserts. Although discussions among politicians are important, we also must engage fossil fuel CEOs so that actual change occurs. Constructive, international action in this area, such as The Hague Principles for a Universal Declaration on Responsibilities for Human Rights and Earth Trusteeship and the Intergovernmental Panel on Climate Change (IPCC), are steps in the right direction. But we need to act from the heart and do much more—and we need to do it much more quickly than we already are.

MOVING TOWARD A DECENTRALIZED SOCIETY

While nation-states and supranationals are competing to realize their respective versions of a unipolar world, a geopolitical push in the opposite direction—i.e., toward decentralization as opposed to centralization—also is occurring. From the perspective of the survival of the entire species, decentralization is much more robust than centralization, since decentralization offers multiple areas of redundancy. Just as biodiversity in crops ensures that if one crop fails, others can fill the gap, a decentralized world helps the whole remain resilient in the face of unanticipated events while providing a way for the whole to manifest in multiple, creative ways.

As systems become larger, they generally become more susceptible to catastrophic failure and collapse (Andresen 2023b, 14; see also Knorr 2020; WPR2022). To avoid global collapse and foster the long-term survival of *Homo sapiens sapiens*, we need a world that is decentralized geopolitically, economically, logistically, and culturally. Essentially, decentralization is an exchange of center and periphery, with hierarchies giving way to decentralized modes of social organization.

A salient question is how much decentralization is ideal—since it would not be optimal to return to an extreme version of multipolarity in which overlapping authorities and allegiances begin to resemble the power dynamics and geopolitical order present in Europe during medieval times. McFate (2014) describes that more dystopian version of multipolarity, namely a polycentric environment in which multiple entities —e.g., transnational corporations, global governing bodies, non-governmental organizations (NGOs), regional and ethnic interests, terror organizations, and even drug cartels—complete with the authority of the nation-state. Accordingly, discerning how much multipolarity is best for human society as a whole is an important task, one that should be pursued with genuineness and sincerity.

DE-DOLLARIZATION
AND SOCIAL JUSTICE

The current, global economic and financial system privileges very wealthy countries. Historically, these are the imperialist countries such as England, France, Belgium, the Netherlands, Spain, Portugal, Germany, Italy, the U.S., Japan, and Turkey, which all in their own ways colonized the global South (GER 2023). The countries of the global South have been trapped in debt for decades, in no small part because of actions taken by the U.S.-dominated World Bank. The World Bank was created in July 1944 in Bretton Woods, New Hampshire, and ever since, many of its policies have favored the U.S. to the detriment of people living in poor countries. Once countries are trapped in debt, the USG has imposed conditionalities that compel these countries to implement the so-called Washington Consensus, which consists of ten economic policy prescriptions promoted by Washington-based institutions such as the International Monetary Fund (IMF), the World Bank, and the U.S. Department of the Treasury. These policy prescriptions are part of a standard reform package that is foisted on developing countries that are struggling economically and, often, politically. The 'standard package' includes a series of neoliberal economic reforms such as mass privatization by selling off state assets, cutting protections for workers, reducing the minimum wage, and decreasing spending for health and education (GER 2023).

In 1974, Saudi Arabia—which is the world's largest oil exporter and historically has been one of the most important U.S. allies—agreed to sell its crude oil in U.S. dollars and invest its oil revenue in U.S. Treasury securities. In return, Saudi Arabia was promised protection by the U.S. government. According to the so-called petrodollar system, the U.S. buys oil from Saudi Arabia and provides the Saudis with military aid and equipment. In return, the Saudis put billions of their petrodollar revenue back into U.S. Treasuries to finance U.S. spending (Wong 2016).

According to the current petrodollar system, Saudi Arabia buys enormous numbers of U.S.-manufactured weapons because of petrodollar recycling—which refers to how U.S. dollars that are expended by the U.S. to purchase oil are recycled back to the U.S. using weapons contracts. These contracts exist between the Saudis and U.S. weapons manufacturers and defense contractors such as Lockheed, Boeing, Raytheon, General Dynamics, and others (Amadeo 2022).

At the time the deal between the U.S. and Saudi Arabia was reached, the petrodollar system was seen as imperative to maintaining the financial health of the U.S., since people did not want to provide the former Soviet Union with an opening it could use to make further inroads into the Arab world. The petrodollar system helps maintain the status of the U.S. dollar as the global reserve currency, and it also helps to finance the U.S. trade deficit and the U.S. current account deficit. The arrangement was meant to neutralize crude oil as an economic weapon and to find a way to persuade the Saudi kingdom—which was perceived as hostile at the time the system was created—to finance the U.S. by means of its newfound petrodollar wealth (Wong 2016).

After U.S. President Richard Nixon ended the convertibility of the dollar to gold in 1971, the petrodollar system helped undergird the status of the U.S. dollar as the global reserve currency. Now, however, the BRICS, which are benefiting from global economic changes, have come together to develop what they see as a fairer system of monetary exchange that would challenge, and ultimately weaken, the dominance of the dollar. Now, however, the new financial institutions of the global South are fracturing the previous financial architecture of the international economic system, which has been dominated for decades by the U.S., and which BRICS members claim privileges very wealthy countries (Norton 2023).

Elimination of the petrodollar system would have massive repercussions for the global financial system. Already, plans by the BRICS to replace the U.S. dollar are causing uncertainty in currency markets. On March 31, 2023, Russian President Vladimir Putin adopted a new foreign policy that identifies China and India as Russia's main allies. According to this new foreign policy, Russia, China, India, and other BRICS countries will create a new currency, in part to ameliorate the negative impact on Russia's economy of Western sanctions and other restrictions resulting from its role in the war in Ukraine. The new medium for payments will not defend either the U.S. dollar or the euro. Instead, it will be secured using gold and other commodities such as rare-earth elements. Russia announced its new foreign policy less than two weeks after President Xi Jinping of the People's Republic of China visited Moscow to further cement the "no limits" partnership that Russia and China announced in 2022. Russia also announced that it will prioritize and enhance its role in groupings such as BRICS so that the world can adapt to a multipolar world (Mitra 2023).

One of the largest factors shifting global macroeconomics today is that China has stated it will purchase Persian Gulf energy, i.e., oil and gas, using China's own currency, the Chinese yuan renminbi (CNY). This topic has been discussed by Xi and top officials from the Gulf monarchies (absolute monarchies Saudi Arabia and Oman, constitutional monarchies Qatar, Kuwait, and Bahrain, and federal monarchy the United Arab Emirates, or UAE) (Norton 2023). As both Saudi Arabia and the BRICS in general are moving toward de-dollarization, Saudi Arabia for example has acknowledged that it is considering selling its crude in other currencies, not only in the U.S. dollar (Wong 2016).

As the world becomes more multipolar, the status of the U.S. dollar as the global reserve currency is being challenged. In fact, even since the end of the Cold War in 1991, historical shifts impacting the global financial system have begun to challenge U.S. hegemonic control of the global reserve system. Although the petrodollar system historically has helped maintain the status of the U.S. dollar as the global reserve currency—since Saudi Arabia has sold its oil in dollars and held its revenues in U.S. Treasuries since 1974—the Saudi's recent interest in de-dollarizing evidenced by its public confirmation that it is considering selling oil in other currencies is a major challenged to the U.S. (GER 2023).

Active talks between Saudi Arabia and China to price some oil sales in CNY is a direct and serious challenge to the petrodollar system. In December 2022, Xi Jinping visited Riyadh, Saudi Arabia, where he met with the Gulf Cooperation Council (GCC) and the twenty-one member states of the Arab League (Norton 2023; see also Said and Kalin 2022). Xi stated that he and top officials from the monarchies listed above discussed purchasing Persian Gulf energy with the CNY, and that China would use its Shanghai exchange for CNY energy deals with Gulf nations. Xi stated:

> China will continue to import large quantities of crude oil from GCC countries, expand imports of liquefied natural gas, strengthen cooperation in upstream oil and gas development, engineering services, storage, transportation and refining, and make full use of the Shanghai Petroleum and Natural Gas Exchange as a platform to carry out yuan settlement of oil and gas trade (Reuters 2022).

China already is Saudi Arabia's top trading partner, and both countries together with others in the GCC have pledged to deepen multilateral trade (Norton 2023).

Unsurprisingly, pushback from the U.S. has arisen over the idea that the CNY will be used to price oil—so the shift may (Kennedy 2023) or may not (Blas 2023) come to pass—or if it does occur, it may not happen immediately. Nevertheless, the fact that Saudi Arabia is engaging in talks with China to price some of its oil in CNY changes the historical relationship between the U.S. and Saudi Arabia, which previously functioned as a client regime of the U.S. (Said and Kalin 2022). Meanwhile, as Saudi Arabia builds a long-term partnership with China despite U.S. security concerns, this will change the composition of major networks of countries. For example, Saudi Arabia's cabinet recently approved that country's decision to join the Shanghai Cooperation Organization (SCO) (Reuters 2023). The SCO is a collective security alliance comprised of eight countries—China, Russia, India, Pakistan, Kazakhstan, Kyrgyzstan, Tajikistan, and Uzbekistan. Iran and Belarus are expected to join by 2024, and, as just mentioned, Saudi Arabia's cabinet recently approved its decision to join.

As the role of the U.S. dollar as global reserve currency diminishes, fewer central banks will invest in U.S. Treasuries. Not only does Saudi Arabia help maintain the hegemony of the U.S. dollar as the global reserve currency when it sells its oil in the U.S. dollar as one aspect of the petrodollar system, but Saudi Arabia also invests the U.S. dollars it makes from oil sales by buying U.S. Treasury securities. This is a major reason that consistent demand has been maintained for U.S. Treasuries over decades, and it has helped the U.S. maintain a constant trade deficit and current account deficit. Now, however, if the petrodollar is challenged, the U.S. loses this advantage according to which it continuously imports more than the rest of the world while running the most egregious deficits—which primarily are military deficits, not deficits accrued to support social programs, healthcare, and edition. Recall that the Pentagon has failed every audit to which it has been subjected, yet Congress continues to allow DOD to amass trillions of dollars in unaccounted for spending. With China's central bank currently investing more in gold reserves, China too has less structural need for U.S. Treasuries. Russia also is investing more in gold for its foreign exchange reserves. Since fewer countries are purchasing treasuries in general, there is less overall demand for U.S. Treasuries in specific. This has major implications for monetary policy. If the Federal Reserve does not print the difference between what foreign countries such as China purchased in the past and what they no longer need to buy need to buy—because for example China does not need to store as many Treasuries as compared to previously—then the dollar 'goes to the moon,' so to speak, and U.S. Treasury yields start going up (GER 2023; see also LG 2023).

In its large-scale effort to create new payment mechanisms to help the global South, BRICS also is challenging the dominance of the U.S. dollar. When it created the New Development Bank (NDB) in 2014, BRICS began a process to provide new sources of financing for the global South that do not have the same political conditionalities as U.S.-imposed structural adjustment does (GER 2023).

When the NDB was created in 2014 by the BRICS as an alternative to the U.S.-dominated World Bank, the focus on creating fairer institutional systems of monetary exchange was front and center (Norton 2023). These new processes introduced by the NDB challenge the U.S.-dominated World Bank, the policies of which often have hurt the global South—since devaluing the currencies in relation to the U.S. dollar of the countries of the global South makes it much more difficult for those countries to import commodities such as oil, gas, and certain foods as part of international trade invoiced in the U.S. dollar. As the U.S. dollar appreciates against other currencies, it also becomes more difficult for countries with debt denominated in U.S. dollars to pay the debt off. It therefore is unsurprising that the countries of the global South want to use the NDB to create a fairer system of monetary exchange while also creating payment mechanisms that do not involve the U.S. dollar (GER 2023). Relatedly, criticism of the U.S.' imposition of unilateral sanctions by South Africa's Foreign Minister Naledi Pandor and others also resonates with countries of the global South. Illegal under international law, unilateral sanctions often negatively impact countries that fall outside a particular conflict (Norton 2023).

Historic developments in the BRICS and Saudi Arabia are part of an international shift to a multipolar economic order (Norton 2023). These and related geopolitical changes are part of a global transition from the unipolar era that has existed since the end of the Cold War to a new, multipolar system. In the unipolar model, the U.S. was the hegemon, the economic order was characterized by globalization, and the U.S. dollar was the currency of choice. Now, however, China is unveiling a new type of globalization via its Belt and Road Initiative (BRI), while BRICS and the emerging economies of the global South are banding together. Meanwhile, the Shanghai Cooperation Organisation (SCO) is growing in size. China understands that it can realize its own objectives more easily by developing ties with Russia and Iran. For example, its relationship with Russia helps China extend its BRI using Arctic shipping lanes. In addition, by participating for the first time in a summit with the Gulf Cooperation Council (GCC) in late 2022, China deepened its ties with OPEC+, i.e., the thirteen core members of OPEC plus another ten, non-OPEC, oil-producing countries that includes Russia, Mexico, and Kazakhstan (Pozsar 2023).

Many outcomes are possible as the world moves from a unipolar to a multipolar mode. If the G20 fractures into two camps—namely the G7 (the U.S., U.K., Canada, France, Germany, Italy, and Japan) plus Australia, on one hand, and BRICS and the non-aligned, on the other—such a massive rift will have a significant impact on the international monetary system. In addition, risks from such a rift are even further intensified by increasing macroeconomic imbalances in the U.S. The dollar-based monetary order is already being challenged in multiple ways, such as the spread of de-dollarization efforts and the creation of central bank digital currencies (CBDCs) (Pozsar 2023).

Although above, I discuss how recent actions by China, Russia, the BRICS more generally, and Saudi Arabia are contributing to de-dollarization, in point of fact, de-dollarization began with the launch of quantitative easing (QE) after the financial crisis of 2007-2008. During that crisis—which sometimes is referred to as the Global Financial Crisis—countries with current account surpluses disapproved of negative real returns on their savings. But now, recent actions by China, Russia, other BRICS countries, and Saudi Arabia have caused the pace of de-dollarization to increase significantly—China and India have begun paying for Russian commodities in CNY, rupees, and UAE dirhams; India is using its new rupee settlement mechanism for its international transactions; and as mentioned briefly above, China has requested that GCC countries make full use of the Shanghai Petroleum and Natural Gas Exchange for CNY settlement of oil and gas trades over the next three to five years. As BRICS expands beyond its current membership, the de-dollarization of trade flows may increase even more (Pozsar 2023).

The effects of CBDCs also are likely to accelerate the de-dollarization of trade flows. China changed the strategy through which it internationalizes the CNY, since it was risky for China to use the same network that Western banks were using to implement financial sanctions via their balance sheets. This is particularly true given that these Western banks form the correspondent banking system that underpins the U.S. dollar. To circumvent Western bank dominance, a new network was required, which, as the IMF has commented, led the central banks of the global East and South in particular to explore and/or to develop digital currents with pilot projects and/or research. The plan is to interlink CBDCs, too. By interlinking central banks by means of CBDCs, something similar to the network of correspondent banks that the U.S. dollar system runs on is created, but with correspondent central banks replacing correspondent banks. This emerging network of CBDCs could enable central banks in the global East and South to serve as foreign exchange dealers to intermediate currency flows between local banking systems. Because the network is enforced with bilateral currency swap lines, one need not reference the U.S. dollar or ever touch the Western banking system—which represents a monumental economic change for the world (Pozsar 2023). It also helps explain why so many countries of the global East and South are interested in joining BRICS.

One immediate impact of the emerging network of CBDCs is that the current account surpluses of China, Russia, and Saudi Arabia—all of which are at a record level—will not be recycled into traditional reserve assets such as U.S. Treasuries, which, at current inflation rates, offer negative real returns. Instead, as mentioned above, China is purchasing gold. In addition, Saudi Arabia plans to invest in commodities such as mining interests and to make investments that are geopolitical in nature, such as funding the BRI and helping allies and neighbors such as Turkey, Egypt, and Pakistan. Increasingly, too, remaining surpluses are being held in liquid form in bank deposits. Since finance depends on marginal flows, which matter the most for the largest marginal borrower—namely the U.S. Treasury—then if less trade is invoiced in U.S. dollars and recycling of dollar surpluses into traditional reserve assets such as U.S. Treasuries decreases, the privilege that the U.S. dollar currently enjoys as the international reserve currency will diminish (Pozsar 2023).

REDISTRIBUTIVE JUSTICE AND DECENTRALIZATION

To live morally, humankind needs to embark on a global, social redistributive justice project. To succeed, a genuine redistributive social justice project requires a return to concepts of 'natural rights' as opposed to orienting society around the idea of 'private property,' as is the case now.

Political systems that permit power to be concentrated at the top are fragile, since they do not support the vast majority of human beings. We already have the technology to support worldwide direct democracy, which means we can start to envision fair and decentralized systems of governance. Even the U.S. has succumbed to too much hierarchy in governance. Because we rely on a representative form of democracy in the U.S., our system retains many elitist elements that one tends to associate with authoritarian governance models. The concentration of wealth, power, and control over resources in the U.S. is increasing, not decreasing, and there is an alarming trend in the U.S. toward more surveillance and increased limitations on civil liberties.

Representative democracy, which depends on hierarchy, leaves too much decision-making in the hands of too few people. One need only consider former U.S. President Donald Trump's essentially unilateral decision to remove the U.S., which obviously is one of the world's largest economies, from the Paris Climate Accord (McGrath 2020). Also unwise are politically organized groups such as PACs (Political Action Committees) and Super PACs, which often concentrate resources to garner support for decisions that favor the socioeconomic elite. Elite interests set the agendas of these groups, which lobby to ensure that policies they favor are enacted. This is the essence of why many laws often do not lead to just outcomes.

Looking far into the future, one can consider how a truly 'intelligent' species might organize itself. Probably absent would be geopolitical constructs such as the nation-state. Models of 'citizenship' are likely to become moot as humankind's movement through spacetime becomes more unencumbered. Perhaps then we will be more like cosmic nomadanauts and less like 'governed' citizens.

To increase social justice, we need to start to decentralize human society. Decentralization fosters creativity by providing people with opportunities. It also supports effective and cooperative local action. Replacing representative democracy with direct democracy would be a good way to start decentralizing governance. Direct democracy is a better model than representative democracy, since it empowers people at all levels of the system. To create a direct democracy in the U.S., we must start by removing the electoral college system. We also need to experiment with methods of direct voting on important issues such as climate initiatives. On global issues, we should experiment with ways to introduce decentralized, blockchain voting across the entire world. This kind of radical democratization of the world's citizens can empower people and create opportunities for everyone.

Decision-making at so-called global institutions such as the United Nations (UN), the Council on Foreign Relations (CFR), the World Bank Group (WBG), and the Bilderberg meetings is even more lopsided in favor of the elite. Perhaps the worst of all possible governance models would be the 'one world government' idea, since it is so vulnerable to corruption and exploitation by the people at the 'top.' At some point, human beings must find the courage to overturn elitist institutions and to create a socially just society. We can start by moving away from hegemonic military initiatives to a multipolar world of functioning nation-states.

Over the long run, even more decentralization probably will prove optimal.

Meanwhile, dysfunctional legal systems must be replaced with consensus models for dispute resolution that are supported by blockchain technologies and that are more efficient than trying to settle differences judicially. The courts are notoriously unfair, since concentrated wealth and power continue to influence judicial decisions, which often serve the elite. A major reason the current legal system is unjust is because the rich hire more and, also, more experienced, lawyers, while the poor often are unable to bring a case at all because of the high threshold to entry. The current legal system must be replaced with something much more accessible. 'Smart contracts' based on blockchain and similar technologies can help move human society beyond dispute resolution that currently depends on the antiquated, overburdened, and glacially slow court system, thereby eliminating reliance on cumbersome legal structures and facilitating faster and smoother interactions.

Another shortcoming of the legal system, which also makes it inaccessible, is that justice often is circumvented when word games are played when laws and treaties are drafted. We need a return to simple language in laws and treaties, so they become more accessible and quicker to implement. As humankind begins to acculturate with intelligent extraterrestrial species, complex legal frameworks articulated in human conceptual and linguistic terms will have no value, since they are based on *human* concepts and language and therefore are too limited in scope. Even at an intraspecies level, complex language often divides people rather than uniting them. Using simpler language in our laws and treaties would be much more inclusive.

Often, arguments over the meanings of complex language take the place of actually doing something to fix things. Ecological devastation, the oppression of the poor, and the privatization, commercialization, militarization, and weaponization of space continue apace while people argue about what certain words mean. A prime example of this is the Outer Space Treaty (OST), the most well known UN agreement relating to space, the principles of which govern activities in outer space (UN 2002, 3-8). As described elsewhere (Andresen 2023c), the language of this treaty often is interpreted in ways that belie its original intention.

Even beyond the law and treaty setting, we need to learn to adhere to ethical and more principles voluntarily, without being 'required' to do so. This will enable us to transcend issues of enforceability altogether. Voluntarily doing the right thing results from deciding to create a just and peaceful world, so that as individuals transform their thinking, society transforms, too. One thing that helps here is perceiving more than just explicate order —we also need to perceive and experience what Bohm refers to as the implicate, etc., levels of order, which also are aspects of the whole (Andresen 2023b).

Viewing things from the perspective of the whole flattens dominance hierarchies across all segments of society. Indeed, the entire notion of dominance relies upon the idea that certain elements in a system, including certain human beings, are above, superior to, and/or more entitled than others to territory, resources, power, status, etc. That assumption in turn relies upon the idea that parts are independent of a whole, which is merely an aggregation of these parts. But the whole is much more than an aggregation of parts. It is an infinite expanse of layers of subtlety in which consciousness and matter are completely coterminous with one another—inseparable, as Bohm puts it (Bohm 1990; Andresen 2022b, 296-304, 316-18; Andresen 2023b). In such a reality—which is, in fact, the true nature of our wondrous reality—there is no room to use disingenuous ploys to try to dominate whatever, or whomever, is perceived as 'other.' Such short-term, calculative thinking always backfires. Instead, when individuals, and, ideally, all members of a species, perceive the whole as infinitely valuable in and of itself, then everything works coherently to support the whole.

THE IMPORTANCE OF LOCAL KNOWLEDGE FORMATION

Decentralizing knowledge formation also can improve our ability to understand the nature of reality clearly. Today, the map of disciplines in the academy is quite stable, even across countries that have very different ideologies for governance. In other words, the *cartography* of knowledge is stable across the human species while the geopolitical topography is not. Moreover, disciplinary stability is increasing while geopolitical topography is becoming increasingly chaotic (Andresen 2022a).

Although we tend to take the divisions between academic disciplines for granted, these divisions were created by human beings in the specific historical context of the Western liberal university system. Decentralizing knowledge formation, organization, and transmission will open knowledge to more cultural contexts, which will support people's ability to respond more creatively to challenges.

The issues facing the world today do not follow disciplinary boundaries. Climate change, species extinction, mass migrations, demographic challenges, poverty, widespread, systemic violence, and many other urgent macro issues facing humankind today do not respect divisions between disciplines—nor will they be resolved by one single disciple or another. We need local knowledge to help, just as we need to learn about mutual participation and the whole nature of reality (Andresen 2023b).

Perceiving the whole will lead to institutional disintermediation, not to more centralization. Institutions are based on transactionalism in thought and action. Transactionalism in turn depends on the fundamental misperception that the whole is nothing more than a concatenation of separate and independently existing 'parts.' Removing this misinformation will contribute to institutional disintermediation as more decentralized knowledge formation makes bureaucratic institutions obsolete.

ECONOMIC DECENTRALIZATION SUPPORTS A FAIRER WORLD

The primary components of the economic sphere are the same now as they were decades ago—namely energy, materials (such as the output of mining operations), organization, and control (Quigley 1966). Power and wealth are concentrated because control of energy, materials, and organization is concentrated. However, a decentralized economy is preferable to a centralized one because it can absorb economic shocks more easily and, also, because it is more conducive to greater social justice because it provides more local opportunities for people to make a living.

Money plays a large role in structuring and, most often, constraining, the experiences of people's daily lives. However, it is easy to forget that what most people think of as money today—namely fiat currency—has not been around long in the history of human trading and commerce.

The current financial system, which is based on transactions settled in the currencies of various nation-states, is unstable. Currency markets are subject to significant shocks that often have a horrendous impact on the poor and vulnerable. In addition, global debt is out of control. The debt-to-GDP ratio is over 100% for many countries and over 200% for some (Amoros 2022).

Layers of regulations relating to money—how, to whom, and under what circumstances it can be created and transferred—dampen actual fluidity in the economic space. These market inefficiencies then are exploited by hedge fund managers, investment bankers, asset managers, etc., who profit from financial arbitrage. In addition, people who engage in insider trading find routes to information that others do not have in order to maximize gain for themselves. Markets are not the least bit free in the real sense of the term, and finance is one of the most unlevel playing fields that exists. Add to this money laundering—which is occurring at an almost unfathomable level globally—and it becomes clear that greed is creating cycles of immoral violence that make many people vulnerable and unsafe.

To untangle greed and reverse human impulses toward control and domination, we must cultivate the direct perception and experience of wholeness. Greed and aggressivity in pursuit of one's personal objects derive from a lack of being grounded in the whole, since greed involves the maladaptive impulse to try to regain a sense of inner wholeness by gaining power and control over external things. But if one feels and experiences the wholeness of existence, there is no reason to invade another country, to hoard resources, or to commit acts of violence. The incorrect indulgence of greed only results in a cyclic repetition of desperate grasping after explicate order manifestations. The antidote is the direct perception of wholeness itself. Existence is precious, and we all participate in it together.

Rhetorical manipulation makes many people think that 'democracy' is inextricably linked to 'free market capitalism,' 'free markets,' and 'private enterprise.' In reality, there is little that is 'free' about the global, macroeconomic order. Wealth is inordinately concentrated in the U.S., which shows that democracy and capitalism to do distribute opportunities for economic empowerment equally throughout society. Furthermore, powerful political and economic insiders use media to shape narratives and to create conditions that favor their own concentration of wealth and power.

Current elite, global control of banking, finance, and the money supply (Navidi 2017) is completely unjust. Because the entire system is so centralized, it also introduces considerable risk into human society—since what happens now at a macro level percolates throughout society and touches almost everyone. Nevertheless, those who finance governments—and the governments who let them do it—are using control of the money supply as a way to control people. To that end, the central bank system literally is designed and operated to benefit the elite at the expense of billions of honest people. Elite collusion involving central banks and international bankers does not serve the masses. It serves the elite (Prins 2018; 2022).

Injustice resulting from central bank collusion is well documented. In the context of actions taken by autocrats in the central bank of Japan, i.e., the Bank of Japan, Richard Werner (2003; see also Totten 2003; Oswald 2014; KI 2023) describes the ideological battle between 'free markets' and 'regulation.' Werner documents how Bank of Japan autocrats engaged in actions to create a recession, which caused tremendous suffering for and dislocation of Japanese citizens. Werner also discusses the long history of this type of activity, which has been undertaken by the European Central Bank and by Adolf Hitler's Reichsbank. As Werner points out, nothing inherently says that business cycles must continue or that markets must go down. By decentralizing the financial markets, we can reduce artificial volatility and create a world that works economically for everyone. Such a world is one of radical abundance, not a zero-sum game.

Places such as the City of London, which is a geographically distinct city within the city of wider London, play a major role in perpetuating economic elitism. Economic elitism is a form of economic exceptionalism, which depends on economic individualism in which people act in their own, personal best interests without considering the impact on others. With very little paper trail designed to help them avoid taxes, people collectively hide trillions of dollars in offshore havens such as Guernsey and the Cayman Islands (Independent POV 2018). But focusing on personal wealth and how to preserve it ignores the importance of empathy, compassion, and caring for others.

The bottom line is that to achieve a fair and just global society, we must restructure the entire world economic system. Decentralized finance, or 'defi,' can help, as can other measures to decentralize financial markets and institutions. Decentralization in the economic sphere can help redistribute wealth by making real economic opportunities available to more people, as can a return to a barter-like system of peer-to-peer exchange using blockchain technologies. Cryptocurrencies untether currency from the nation-state, which is a good thing if we really want to support free enterprise.

Moving capital into decentralized, cryptocurrency markets would make everyone less reliant on the banking sector overall, though it would have to occur in sufficiently high volume to overcome the control of big money. Despite visionary work to create a working infrastructure for decentralized finance, the cryptocurrency market continues to mirror asset markets more generally since there is so much big money already invested in crypto. Over the long run, however, as more people worldwide begin to use crypto, the world may be able to realize a genuine, decentralized financial infrastructure (ETHGlobal 2019).

ENDING LAND HOARDING

One of the reasons that monarchy remains one of the most atavistic and socially unjust systems remaining on Earth in the twenty-first century is because it concentrates land ownership in the hands of a few, when so many of the world's people desperately need more space to live and to farm, for example.

The largest non-governmental landowner in the world is the head of the British Commonwealth. This currently is King Charles III, who essentially controls some estimated 2.7 billion hectares of land, or roughly one-sixth of the Earth's land surface. King Charles III also controls 90% of the land in Canada, since Canada is a constitutional monarchy according to which the Sovereign in the U.K. automatically becomes Sovereign of Canada and Canada's formal Head of State. In fact, King Charles III currently is head of state of fifteen nations, including Australia and New Zealand. The land holdings of the British Commonwealth are not 'private property' in the sense one normally thinks of it, but this enormous amount of land is under the control of the British Commonwealth nonetheless.

Land hoarding of the type typified by monarchy is an affront to social justice. The original Patriots in the U.S.—also known as Revolutionaries—were colonists who rebelled against British monarchical control and fought valiantly against inherited power in order to win independence for the Thirteen Colonies. Even though the United States of America was declared an independent nation in July 1776, people today seem oblivious to how monarchies continue to control so much of the world.

Now, not only monarchs but also the supranationals and the ultrarich hoard land. In fact, a major method the elite use to store wealth is to buy real estate and land. Concentration of land ownership is extreme. The total land surface of Earth is approximately 57.3 billion square miles, of which around 35% is desert and 25% are mountains, which leaves more than half of the Earth's surface virtually uninhabitable. Doing some math, there are approximately 16 billion square acres of Earth's surface that are inhabitable. Regarding this area, the top four landowners in the world are: 1) the family of King Charles of Great Britain (6.75 billion acres); 2) the Catholic Church (177 million acres); 3) the Inuit people in Nunavut, Northern Canada (87.5 million acres); and 4) Gina Rinehart, an Australian billionaire mining magnate and businesswoman (22.7 million acres) (Scribner 2023). Meanwhile, the largest private landowner in the U.K. is from Denmark—i.e., Danish billionaire Anders Holch Povlsen, who owns over 220,000 acres in Scotland alone (Picken and Nicholson 2019). Sheikh Mohammed bin Rashid al-Maktoum of Dubai also is reported to have bought approximately 63,000 acres of Scottish land.

Meanwhile, in the U.S., the top four landowners are: 1) the Emmerson family of California, and Sierra Pacific Industries (2.4 million acres); 2) John Carol Malone, the former CEO of Tele-Communications Inc. (2.2 million acres, which is 3,437 square miles, or twice the size of the entire State of Rhode Island); 3) Ted Turner, the founder of CNN (2.2 million acres); and 4) the Reed family of Simpson Investment Company and its spinoff, Green Diamond Resource (1.7 million acres) (O'Keefe 2023). Together, one hundred wealthy families in the U.S. own a whopping *42 million acres of land* (Grant 2019).

Obviously, none of the concentrated land ownership makes any sense from the perspectives of social justice and basic morality. Theoretically, there is no reason that humankind cannot decide to restrict land ownership. We could link land ownership to best use—with 'best' being determined by true, direct, global democracy, empowered by blockchain voting.

If we really want to push the social justice envelope, we can ask if private property of any type really makes sense. The current concept of private property encompasses everything from mineral wealth to intellectual property, which the ultrarich consolidate in financial, media, land, and other holdings. Consolidation of wealth depends upon a legal system that supports the notion of private property in the first place. By now, the notion of private property is so ingrained in people's minds that few people question it—even though the concept of 'property'

was not legally defined in England until the 17th century (Aylmer 1980). If humankind truly wishes to evolve, the entire notion of private property will need to be dismantled. This will require thinking about new notions of value and how to exchange using peer-to-peer technology.

DEVELOPING LOCAL AND REGIONAL TRADING NETWORKS

A more socially just world requires more widespread access to resources, which requires developing local and regional networks for logistics and trade.

Global logistics and exchange networks have become far too interconnected, which makes them vulnerable to shocks, sabotage, and other forms of disruption. The world already has witnessed the devastation caused by sabotage of the Nord Stream and Nord Stream 2 pipelines and the Nord Stream network, for example (Jeffrey Sachs 2023; NCTV 2023; Hersh 2023a; 2023b).

In addition to energy infrastructure, there also are many other potential targets of sabotage, such as sea containers, railways, and trucking networks, which transport goods often over vast distances from one country to another. Especially in the case of food production and distribution, it makes sense to encourage local or at least regional alternatives to this dependence on long-distance transport. In addition, the information technology (IT) systems controlling transportation and electricity grids, etc., also are too centralized, which makes them vulnerable to attacks on sites where hardware is located, and, also, to large-scale hacking and malware attacks. This entire, centralized infrastructure on which society depends for trade in natural resources, energy, food, other goods, and IT needs to be decentralized as urgently as possible.

Control over the world's natural resources is far too concentrated, which often introduces inefficiencies that did not exist when natural resources such as water were shared within a region. After the collapse of the former Soviet Union, for example, cooperation in Central Asia disintegrated significantly between the Stans—i.e., Kazakhstan, Kyrgyzstan, Tajikistan, Turkmenistan, and Uzbekistan (defined here according to the more restricted sense of the term 'Stans,' since a larger region is indicated when one adds Afghanistan and the Xinjiang region of China). When the former Soviet requirements for water sharing disappeared in the Stans, individual countries began to withhold resources from one another and to sell them outside the region to foreign buyers with more money. This resulted in an unprecedented water shortage, which has been exacerbated by climate change caused by a decrease in the flow in the Amu Darya River. Although in the short run, it was more profitable to sell resources outside of the circle, energy prices skyrocketed, and the population and governments of the region were destabilized. In Kyrgyzstan, for example, the rolling blackouts and cutoffs that occurred during the winter of 2009-2010 as energy prices increased were the immediate precedent to the Kyrgyz Revolution of 2010, also known as the Second Kyrgyz Revolution (NTO 2016). Here, the moral of the story is not that countries in the region should return to a Soviet style system with forced water sharing requirements, but, rather, that countries in regions such as Central Asia themselves should make the decision to share resources such as water regionally, regardless of whether more money could be made selling outside the region.

Water is an increasingly contested natural resource, with conflict over water rights increasing worldwide. We need to decentralize the distribution of water, food, and energy, and blockchain technologies can assist with this. With respect to water, for example, blockchain can direct resources toward the development of desalination and other technologies to make water drinkable. With respect to food, blockchain can help with developing vertical farming. Decentralization of water, food, and energy can empower people so they are not required to negotiate with governments and private companies to obtain necessities.

THE DECENTRALIZING, GLOBAL IMPACT OF ETI/UAP

In many of my other publications (Andresen 2021; 2022a; 2022b; 2023b; 2023c; 2024), I discuss the ongoing process of creative acculturation with an advanced Extraterrestrial Intelligence (ETI) operating Unidentified Anomalous Phenomena (UAP) on and around Earth. With respect to the topic of the centralization versus decentralization of human society, my view is that increasing acculturation with ETI will have a decentralizing impact on human society as a whole, and it will lead to a more decentralized global economy, with less centralized control over the money supply. Rapid disintermediation and de-institutionalization also is likely to occur as governance, money, commerce, and logistics become less subject to centralized control. In addition, geopolitics will become less conflictual, and narratives surrounding ETI will become more cooperative.

With respect to ETI and the economy, we should not promote the idea in people's minds that the confirmation by a major nation-state that some UAP are extraterrestrial in origin will negatively impact financial markets. Some commentators already have begun to suggest that extraterrestrial UAP are economically disruptive. The reasoning is that if countries and militaries are uncertain about the capabilities of extraterrestrial UAP, and if this uncertainty were widely acknowledged, that financial markets would respond negatively (Kaminska 2021). A similar idea is that if concern about UAP grows, it could contribute to current instability in the banking sector, including in the U.S. (Karaian and Cowley 2023) and in China (Gan 2022).

Unfortunately, some supranational special interests are

expending unnecessary energy trying to suggest that ETI/UAP are a 'threat,' or otherwise 'dangerous' in some way. At least in part, this threat narrative has its origins in the discussions held by a group of people who repeatedly crop up in the history of UFOs/UAP, from the 1980s to the present day (Basterfield 2019). But there is no need to feed such paranoia, which is completely antithetical to more constructive participation with ETI (Andresen 2022b; 2023). It makes much more sense to speak reassuringly and to advocate for calm.

Economist Paul Krugman apparently made a dystopian joke that additional investment in defense technologies could be fast-tracked to "defend humanity from a foreign alien invasion," and that "it might be worth conducting a hoax to draw such effects in their own right." Despite this being a horrific and unethical idea, people are in fact starting to identify UAP portfolio risk. At least one Wall Street product, the Procure Space ETF, actively attempts to account for financial risk associated with UAP. The Fund's Prospectus states that because there is no current identification of these observed phenomena, that UAP could interfere either unintentionally or deliberately with satellites and other objects in space at operational, data security, and/or cyber levels. Such interference adversely would impact the securities in the Fund, states the Prospectus. This would cause the Fund's investment in such portfolio securities to lose value and would adversely impact the Fund's ability to fulfill its investment objectives (Kaminska 2021).

If one human group were to obtain UAP technology ahead of others, it could destabilize the global balance of power, disrupt trade in goods and services, and cause the global financial system to collapse suddenly. Almost everyone would suffer. Alternatively, if humankind matured ethically and spiritually enough so that useful knowledge from extraterrestrial technology could be disseminated without concerns that the information would be weaponized (Andresen 2023b), then massive real wealth would be injected into the global system. Regardless, the road may be rocky as free energy systems begin to replace fossil fuels. It therefore is imperative that people think carefully about how to make such a transition—when the time is right, etc.—so financial markets are not unduly disrupted.

Creative acculturation with ETI will have profound implications for the energy sector of the global economy (Andresen 2023b, 170-74). Extraterrestrial UAP appear to have access to abundant, clean energy and to utilize advanced propulsion that does not depend upon a petroleum-based liquid propellant or any other conventional rocket propulsion system. Instead, a different method of overcoming gravity and achieving lift is involved. If abundant energy were to become available to human beings on a virtually unlimited scale, reliance on fossil fuels and any currency system involved with their trade, such as the petrodollar system, would cease to be relevant. The elite who currently profit from energy production in the oil and natural gas sectors would see themselves sidelined if a different sort of 'free' energy were to become widely available—unless of course it controlled this new energy source.

ETI AND SPIRITUALITY

Greater creative acculturation with ETI will lead to massive changes in spirituality. Largescale, centralized religions most likely will become less popular as people seek out more personal, spiritual encounters. Mystical experience and other types of direct, religious experience that rely on embodied knowledge will become more popular as fundamentalist religious views decrease.

Mystical experience, which is compatible with metaphor, analogy, and eschewal of a materialist reductionist approach to reality, is deeply compatible with local knowledge. People who follow a more normative, fundamentalist view of religion tend to think in a manner that is more literal and concrete, i.e., a kind of materialist reductionist view despite the spiritual metanarrative on top of it. Relying on the concrete words of religious texts to guide their actions, those who approach religion and spirituality using a fundamentalist lens almost always rely on other people, many of whom are manipulative, to interpret religious texts for them. This then often leads to acts of religious intolerance and violent extremism.

Although some academics have tried to explain the rise of religious fanaticism and violent extremism by referring to anthropological explanations such as the influence of kin networks and by referring to sociological explanations such as response to uncertainty—or even by referring to economic explanations such as the need and/or desire to amass money and control resources—the reality is that even when world leaders invade other countries, they sometimes are motivated by more than a purely cynical desire for personal economic gain. Often part of the motivation to invade also carries a religious overtone, as one can see in Putin's thinking as it relates to Ukraine. Be that as it may, neither materialist fundamentalism nor idealism is compatible with the deeper and more correct understanding that matter and consciousness are inseparable (Bohm 1990; Andresen 2022b; 2023).

As creative acculturation with ETI unfolds, many human meaning narratives will be impacted by new perceptions and understandings regarding the nature of reality. Some of these will involve religion and theology. Indeed, the Vatican is trying to prepare for this already. The Vatican has shown itself to be open to the possible existence of life elsewhere in the universe, and it supports discussions on the ethical and theological implications of widespread participation with extraterrestrials. In fact, the Vatican Press Office already has issued a pontifical press statement relating to Contact (capitalized here to indicate Contact across essentially the entire human population) (Pope Francis 2014; Losch and Krebs 2015). The Vatican Observatory also boasts a large collection of writings on the topic of life in the universe and on ETI that is available on its website (Vatican Observatory n.d.; 2016).

A recent study examines Catholic responses to ETI (Thigpen 2022). Specific comments on ETI also have been made by two astronomers who have served as Director of the Vatican Observatory. Astronomer José Gabriel Funes, SJ, was interviewed by Francesco M. Valiante in 2008 when Funes was Director of the Vatican Observatory about Funes' views on ETI. Funes, who uses a warm, familial tone throughout the interview, discusses commonalities between species and expresses an open and welcoming attitude toward ETI (Funes 2008).

Funes proposes that we view ETIs as our brothers and sisters. His remarks also reflect his attempt to reconcile a cosmic paradigm that includes extraterrestrial life, including intelligent, extraterrestrial life, with Christianity. Translated from Italian, part of Valiante's interview with Funes follows:

Valiante: But Genesis speaks of the earth, of animals,

of man and woman. Does this exclude the possibility of the existence of other worlds or living beings in the universe?

Funes: In my opinion this possibility [of the existence of other worlds and living beings in the universe] exists. Astronomers believe that the universe consists of one hundred billion galaxies, each of which is composed of one hundred billion stars. Many, or almost all, of these could have planets. How can it be excluded that life has also developed elsewhere? There is a branch of astronomy, astrobiology, which studies precisely this aspect and which has made a lot of progress in recent years. By examining the spectra of light coming from stars and planets, it will soon be possible to identify the elements in their atmospheres —the so-called *biomarkers* [note, original incorrectly writes *biomakers*]—and to understand if there are conditions for the birth and development of life. After all, life forms could theoretically exist even without oxygen or hydrogen.

Valiante: Are you also referring to beings similar to us or more evolved?

Funes: Possibly [they are more evolved]. So far we have no proof. But certainly in such a large universe this hypothesis cannot be excluded.

Valiante: And wouldn't this be a problem for our faith?

Funes: I do not think so. Just as there is a multiplicity of creatures on Earth, so there could be other beings, even intelligent ones, created by God. This does not conflict with our faith, because we cannot place limits on God's creative freedom. In the words of St. Francis, if we consider earthly creatures as our "brother" and "sister," why could we not also speak of an "extraterrestrial brother"? (Italian: *Per dirla con san Francesco, se consideriamo le creature terrene come "fratello" e "sorella", perché non potremmo parlare anche di un "fratello extraterrestre"?*) It would still be part of creation.

Valiante: And what about redemption?

Funes: Let us borrow the Gospel image of the lost sheep. The shepherd leaves ninety-nine in the fold to go look for the one that has been lost. We think that in this universe there may be a hundred sheep, corresponding to different forms of creatures. We who belong to the human race could just be the lost sheep, the sinners who need a shepherd. God became man in Jesus to save us. Thus, even if there were other intelligent beings, it is not said that they should need redemption. They may have remained in full friendship with their Creator.

Valiante: I insist: If instead they were sinners, would redemption also be possible for them?

Funes: Jesus became incarnate once and for all. The incarnation is a unique and unrepeatable event. However, I am sure that they too, in some way, would have the opportunity to enjoy God's mercy, as it was for us men [i.e., humans].

While it is the personal opinion of Funes that the incarnation event is reserved for humankind, Funes also thinks that extraterrestrials would have access to redemption and mercy, if, indeed, they were sinners at all. Funes therefore has found a way to reconcile his personal interpretation of Catholicism with the reality of ETIs.

Br. Guy Consolmagno, SJ. Consolmagno, who succeeded Funes as Director of the Vatican Observatory, similarly articulates a welcoming stance toward ETIs. Consolmagno states that in accordance with the position of Pope Francis, the Catholic Church would baptize an extraterrestrial if the extraterrestrial requested it (Consolmagno and Mueller 2014; Jha 2010; Ohlheiser 2014). Consolmagno (2016) has spoken and written prolifically about ETIs, for example in a video in which he discusses a 'hypothetical' scenario in which ETI comes to Earth. In addition, a booklet authored by Consolmagno begins with his intuition that sooner or later ETI will be discovered, the implications of which he discusses for Catholic belief (Consolmagno 2005).

Certainly, theologians from all faiths will present many different interpretations of how theology can be reconciled with the reality of ETI. Some scholars make a compelling argument that religions that do not subscribe to the idea of a Creator —for example Buddhism—will have less difficulty adapting to the reality of ETI as compared to monotheistic traditions (Huntington 1976).

Indeed, Buddhism indeed is very compatible with the existence of ETI. In many of its manifestations, Buddhism is more of a systematic worldview or philosophy than it is a religion per se, with much of the early Buddhist writing from India being very philosophical in orientation. Many Buddhist philosophical teachings share a heritage that can be traced back to early Pāli and Sanskrit texts that are part of an ancient Vedic and Indo-Tibetan tradition. Many of these texts mention a plethora of advanced, non-human beings who routinely make their appearances on Earth and who actively participate with humankind here. Even though Buddhist writers tended to refer to these beings as divine or semidivine, it is quite plausible that at least some of these beings described in ancient texts were what we call "extraterrestrials" today. Buddhist texts encourage people to adopt a welcoming stance toward these advanced beings.

Over the centuries, as Buddhism was disseminated to other parts of the world such as East Asia, it took on more devotional and religious aspects, especially Chinese Mahāyāna Buddhism. Interestingly, although China is not explicitly Buddhist, the country sometimes is symbolized by the divine dragon. This dragon figure is sacred to many people at all levels of Chinese society, leading some people to speculate that dragon symbolism —which is found across the world—may be an artistic rendering of UAP as 'dragons.'

Looking back through the centuries and including input from different cultural contexts helps us understand that human interaction with ETI may be the norm, not the exception. People who are religious in orientation can find reassurance from the fact that many theologians do not think there is any reason to be afraid of our extraterrestrial neighbors. I agree. In addition, many theologians and other religious leaders recognize the importance of humanity's entrance into a community of cosmic cultures.

Even though the hermeneutics underlying most theologies are robust enough to handle ETI without requiring much revision, over time, I think a combined physics/phenomenology approach to ontology will end up supplanting both theology and science as the process of creative acculturation with ETI unfolds (Andresen in preparation; see also Andresen 2024).

WELCOMING ETI AS OUR NEIGHBOR

As I discuss elsewhere (Andresen 2023a), from the perspectives of both physics and of evolutionary biology, a sophisticated ETI will have evolved to be altruistic. Accordingly, both a physics perspective and also an evolutionary biology one make it abundantly clear that the ETI in our midst now is well intentioned toward humankind.

ETI has been participating with humankind for a long time. Even though many indigenous and other, non-Western cultures such as those of India and Tibet have been aware of this fact for generations, many people in the contemporary West are only awakening to this reality now. The history of ETI/UAP interactions with human beings buttresses the view that ETI is well-intentioned toward humankind.

For at least over a thousand years, ETI/UAP have acted in a helpful manner toward human beings. This is true even given that ETI possesses vastly superior technology as compared to that possessed by humans, which means that ETI easily could have dominated and/or destroyed human society if it had wanted to do so. Obviously, this has not occurred. Instead, ETI stands by patiently and continues to try to help (Andresen 2021; 2022b; 2023).

Buttressed by Bohm's framework, we can conclude that **ETI/UAP are not a threat to humankind**. Not only is this true of any ETI/UAP that have reached Earth already, it also is true of any ETI/UAP that will reach Earth in the future. To travel interstellar or intergalactic distances, any ETI requires a knowledge of physics that recognizes unbroken wholeness. Such 'breakthrough perception,' which is benevolent and compassionate, is necessary to master the amount of energy necessary for travel over vast distances without obliterating one's own species by means of the immense amount of energy required (Andresen 2022b; 2023). Breakthrough perception therefore must come before breakthrough propulsion is safe for any species to pursue (Andresen 2023a).

Furthermore, ETI's understanding of and ability to operationalize implicate, super-implicate, etc., levels of order further reinforces its kindness, *because the very nature of these higher levels of order is benevolence and compassion* (Andresen 2023a). As mentioned above, Bohm says of super-implicate order that one can propose it is something that is benevolent and compassionate, not neutral or negative (Bohm 1986, 40). Grasping the ontology of wholeness, and understanding that the survival and prospering of all species is enhanced when species cooperate as part of larger groups, the ETI in our midst now has evolved toward cooperativeness and patience and is trying to teach human beings about the benefits of cooperation over conflict.

Becoming aware of ETI's kind and gentle nature will help human beings cultivate and embody a cooperative disposition toward ETI, with whom we can participate in a process of creative acculturation as with any spiritual friend (Skt. *kalyāṇamitra*). The universe is vast and abundant, and it is our shared home. Embodying a disposition of kindness will help us realize true security and sustainability for our own species, for other species, for Earth, and for the whole.

Fortunately, many individuals and governments of the world see the positive benefits of communication with ETI. In December 2007, for example, in Japan, policy discussions occurred on "Extraterrestrial Policy and Earth Changes." The Japanese and international media reported widely on these discussions, during which key members of the Japanese government engaged in a public discussion relating to public policy toward extraterrestrial civilizations (ETCs), with many participants voicing a positive approach. During a news conference after the event, Japanese Defence Minister Shigeru Ishiba issued a very constructive statement in which he noted that under the terms of Japan's pacifist constitution, if extraterrestrials were to land in peace, there would be no legal grounds on which Japan would attack them. He stated at the time, "There are debates over what makes UFOs fly, but it would be difficult to say it's an encroachment of air space" (Reuters Staff 2007). Even though our extraterrestrial neighbors may have migrated to Earth from elsewhere in the universe, many may live here now as residents of our immediate environment.

To encourage people to develop a kind and constructive approach toward the ETI in our midst now, I like to refer to this ETI as a friend and neighbor. I like the terms friend and neighbor because they mitigate against conceptual distinctions between 'us' and 'them' at both practical and ontological levels. Practically, even within the human species, 'us versus them' scenarios often have tragic and devastatingly violent consequences. It is important that we must overcome such divisive thinking while we also learn to participate constructively with ETI. Furthermore, at a deeper ontological level, no absolute distinction exists between any being. There are no independently existing 'selves.' Instead, we are all part of the whole.

By assuming a friendly, welcoming stance toward ETI and taking an internal locus of control stance, everyone can participate in creative acculturation with ETI in a self-aware and personal way. The more open we are as human beings, the more quickly creative acculturation with ETI will unfold. Someday, humankind may reach the point when we can join a galactic or even intergalactic network of intelligent civilizations.

For now, we should recall that the universe is a very big place, and there is no reason to be afraid. We share the universe with all ETIs, and it is the home for all of us. Differences between species have very little meaning given that we all exist within the same, entangled reality. We therefore should resist any temptation to reify humankind as one 'species' and our extraterrestrial neighbors as some sort of 'ultimate Other,' since doing so only would function to indulge a false, biological essentialism. Instead of taking that path, which is paranoid to the extreme, human beings should embrace the fact that ultimately, all species are related and all participate in the same whole.

To the extent that we can listen carefully to what ETI is communicating, and to the extent that we can communicate constructively ourselves, creative participation with ETI will accelerate and take on even more splendid manifestations. Now is the time to try to participate with ETI with kindness, compassion, wisdom, and love.

REFERENCES

Alcorn, Chauncey. 2020. "US billionaires' fortunes have skyrocketed $845 billion since March." *CNN*, September 17, 2020. https://www.cnn.com/2020/09/17/business/us-billionaire-wealth-increase-pandemic/index.html.

Amadeo, Kimberly. 2022. "What Is the Petrodollar?" The Balance, June 4, 2022. https://www.thebalance.com/what-is-a-petrodollar-3306358.

Amoros, Raul. 2022. "Visualizing the State of Global Debt, by Country." Visual Capitalist, February 1, 2022. https://www.visualcapitalist.com/global-debt-to-gdp-ratio/.

Andresen, Jensine. 2023a. *Bohm's Interpretation of the Quantum Theory: Implications for Extraterrestrial Intelligence (ETI) and Unidentified Anomalous Phenomena (UAP)*. Kindle Direct Publishing.

———. 2023b. *Extraterrestrial Ethics*. London: Ethics Press.

———. In preparation. *Extraterrestrial Mind*.

———. 2022a. "Cartographies of Knowledge and Academic Maps." In *Extraterrestrial Intelligence: Academic and Societal Implications*, edited by Jensine Andresen and Octavio A. Chon Torres, 2-6. Newcastle upon Tyne, U.K.: Cambridge Scholars Publishing.

———. 2022b. "Mind of the Mater, Matter of the Mind." In *Extraterrestrial Intelligence: Academic and Societal Implications*, edited by Jensine Andresen and Octavio A. Chon Torres, 281-330. Newcastle upon Tyne, U.K.: Cambridge Scholars Publishing.

———. 2023c. *Safe Space: Demilitarizing Space for Humans and*

Extraterrestrials. Kindle Direct Publishing.

———. 2021. "Two Elephants in the Room of Astrobiology." In *Astrobiology: Science, Ethics, and Public Policy*, edited by Octavio A. Chon Torres, Ted Peters, Joseph Seckbach, and Richard Gordon, 193-231. Hoboken, NJ/Beverly MA, Wiley/Scrivener.

———. 2024. "Which Science?" in *Astroanthropology: Science, Ethics, and Religion*, edited by Arvin Gouw, Brian Patrick Green, Junghyung Kim, and Ted Peters.

Aylmer, Gerald E. 1980. "The Meaning and Definition of 'Property' in Seventeenth-Century England." *Past and Present* 86, no. 1 (February): 87-97. Oxford: Oxford University Press. https://academic.oup.com/past/article-abstract/86/1/87/1588090?redirectedFrom=fulltext.

Basterfield, Keith. 2019. "The Advanced Theoretical Physics Project – documents from their first meeting." Unidentified Aerial Phenomena – scientific research, June 24, 2019. https://ufos-scientificresearch.blogspot.com/search/label/ATP.

Batstone, David, Eduardo Mendieta, Lois Ann Lorentzen, and Dwight N. Hopkins. 1997. *Liberation Theologies, Postmodernity, and the Americas*. London/New York: Routledge.

Bensaid, Adam. 2019. "Two American billionaires and their shady deals with Israeli intelligence." *TRT World*, 2019. https://www.trtworld.com/magazine/two-american-billionaires-and-their-shady-deals-with-israeli-intelligence-28819.

BIS (Bank of International Settlements). 2022. "About BIS – overview." BIS, December 14, 2022. https://www.bis.org/about/index.htm#:~:text=Established%20in%201930%2C%20the%20BIS,about%2095%25%20of%20world%20GDP.

———. n.d.-a. "Board of Directors." BIS. https://www.bis.org/about/board.htm?m=2002.

———. n.d.-b. "History – overview. BIS. https://www.bis.org/

about/history.htm.

Bittner, Jochen. 2018. "Who Will Win the New Great Game?" *The New York Times*, April 26, 2018. https://www.nytimes.com/2018/04/26/opinion/russia-china-west-power.html.

Blas, Javier. 2023. "The Myth of the Inevitable Rise of a Petroyuan." Opinion. *Bloomberg*, February 27, 2023. https://www.bloomberg.com/opinion/articles/2023-02-27/pricing-petroleum-in-china-s-yuan-sounds-inevitable-not-for-saudi-arabia?leadSource=uverify%20wall.

Bocedi, Alessio, Giovanni Romanelli, Carla Andreani, and Roberto Senesi. 2020. "Hydrogen nuclear mean kinetic energy in water down the Mariana Trench: Competition of pressure and salinity." *The Journal of Chemical Physics* 153, no. 13 (October 6). https://pubs.aip.org/aip/jcp/article-abstract/153/13/134306/199470/Hydrogen-nuclear-mean-kinetic-energy-in-water-down?redirectedFrom=fulltext.

Bohm, David J. 1986. "The implicate order and the super-implicate order." In *Dialogues with Scientists and Sages: The Search for Unity*, edited by Renée Weber, 23-49. London and New York: Routledge & Kegan Paul.

———. 1989. "Meaning and Information." In *The Search for Meaning: The New Spirit in Science and Philosophy*, edited by Paavo Pylkkänen, 43-62. Wellingborough, UK: Crucible. [Page numbers refer to the PDF of Bohm's chapter available at https://www.implicity.org/Downloads/Bohm_meaning+information.pdf.]

———. 1990. "A new theory of the relationship of mind and matter." *Philosophical Psychology* 3, no. 2: 271-86. https://dl.icdst.org/pdfs/files/05aaa28b931575ca2e0baeadc5ab0d2c.pdf.

Brumfiel, Geoff. 2021. "A New Tunnel

Is Spotted At A Chinese Nuclear Test Site *https://www.npr.org/2021/07/30/1022209337/a-new-tunnel-is-spotted-at-a-chinese-nuclear-test-site*, July 30, 2021. https://www.npr.org/2021/07/30/1022209337/a-new-tunnel-is-spotted-at-a-chinese-nuclear-test-site.

Campden. 2023. "Some of Europe's Wealthiest Families Join Forces to Take the Rothschild & Co Bank Private." Campden FB, February 15, 2023. https://www.campdenfb.com/article/some-europe-wealthiest-families-join-forces-take-rothschild-co-bank-private.

Chen, Stephen. 2021. "China military uses AI to track rapidly increasing UFOs." *South China Morning Post*, June 4, 2021. https://www.scmp.com/news/china/science/article/3136078/china-military-uses-ai-track-rapidly-increasing-ufos.

Consolmagno, Guy. 2016. "Extraterrestrial Life." https://youtu.be/7Y3N4lbyM20.

———. 2005. *Intelligent Life in the Universe? Catholic belief and the search for extraterrestrial intelligent life.* Catholic Truth Society, Publishers to the Holy See. https://www.vaticanobservatory.org/wp-content/uploads/2020/10/Intelligent-Life.pdf.

Consolmagno, Guy, and Mueller, Paul. 2014. *Would You Baptize an Extraterrestrial? ... and Other Questions from the Astronomer's In-box at the Vatican Observatory.* New York: IMAGE [a trademark of Random House LLC].

Devonshire-Ellis, Chris. 2022. "The New Candidate Countries For BRICS Expansion." *Silk Road Briefing*, November 9, 2022. https://www.silkroadbriefing.com/news/2022/11/09/the-new-candidate-countries-for-brics-expansion/.

Dixit, Pranav. 2023. "'Is Ukraine being privatized': Netizens fume over President Zelensky's meet with BlackRock management." *Business Today*, May 6, 2023. https://www.businesstoday.in/latest/world/story/is-ukraine-being-privatised-netizens-fume-over-president-zelenskyys-meet-with-blackrock-management-380295-2023-05-06.

Desjardins, Jeff. 2020. "All of the World's Money and Markets in One Visualization." *Visual Capitalist, May* 27, 2020. https://www.visualcapitalist.com/all-of-the-worlds-money-and-markets-in-one-visualization-2020/.

ETHGlobal. 2019. "'Decentralized finance is going to come first' – Vitalik Buterin at ETHCapeTown," April 19, 2019. https://www.youtube.com/watch?v=1lfG78Fk9ac.

Fields, Gregg. 2013. "The Tower of Institutional Corruption: The Bank for International Settlements In The Nightmare years." Edmond & Lily Safra Center for Ethics, July 2, 2013. https://ethics.harvard.edu/blog/tower-institutional-corruption.

Freeman, Ben, and William D. Hartung. 2023. "Unwarranted Influence, Twenty-First-Century-Style: Not Your Grandfather's Military-Industrial Complex." *TomDispatch*, May 4, 2023. https://tomdispatch.com/unwarranted-influence-twenty-first-century-style/.

Funes, José Gabriel Funes. 2008. "L'extraterrestre è mio fratello."

Interview by Francesco M. Valiante. *L'Osservatore romano*, May

14, 2008. https://www.vatican.va/news_services/or/or_quo/

interviste/2008/112q08a1.html.

Gan, Nectar. 2022. "China crushes mass protest by bank depositors demanding their life savings back." *CNN*, July 11, 2022. https://www.cnn.com/2022/07/10/china/china-henan-bank-depositors-protest-mic-intl-hnk/index.html.

GER (Geopolitical Economy Report). 2023. "BRICS challenge US dollar, Saudi considers selling oil in other currencies: Financial multipolarity." January 21, 2023. https://www.youtube.com/watch?v=ryKuoB9JEBE.

Grant, Conor. 2019. "America's big business billionaires are buying up LOTS of land." *The Hustle*, September 16, 2019. https://thehustle.co/09162019-land-billionaires/.

Hersh, Seymour. 2023a. "From The Gulf of Tonkin To The Baltic Sea: The secret and incomplete history of US-Norway collaboration in covert operations." Substack, February 22, 2023. https://seymourhersh.substack.com/p/from-the-gulf-of-tonkin-to-the-baltic?utm_source=%2Fsearch%2FRobert%2520Baer&utm_medium=reader2.

———. 2023b. "How America Took Out The Nord Stream Pipeline." Substack, February 8, 2023. https://seymourhersh.substack.com/p/how-america-took-out-the-nord-stream.

Huntington, Ronald. 1976. "Mything the Point: ETIs in a Hindu/Buddhist Context." In *Extra-Terrestrial Intelligence: The First Encounter*, edited by James L. Christian. Buffalo, NY: Prometheus Books.

Independent POV. 2018. *The Spider's Web: Britain's Second Empire | Documentary Film.* September 14, 2018. https://www.youtube.com/watch?v=np_ylvc8Zj8&t=6s.

Jeffrey Sachs. 2023. Jeffrey Sacs on the Nord Stream Investigation |UN Security council|. February 23, 2023. https://www.youtube.com/watch?v=OZyjFUXXGBA.

Jencks, Charles. 1996. *What is Post-Modernism?* Runnemede, NJ: Academy Press.

Jha, Alok. 2010. "Pope's astronomer says he would baptise an alien if it asked him." *The Guardian*, September 17, 2010. https://www.theguardian.com/science/2010/sep/17/pope-astronomer-baptise-aliens.

Johnson, David W. 2022. *Aligning Megalithic Sites of Southern England and Carnac, France with Groundwater Features: Aligning the Three Worlds.* Rhinebeck, NY: Monkfish Book Publishing Company.

Jung, Carl G. 2006 <1957, 1958>. *The Undiscovered Self.* Translated from the German by R.F.C. Hull. New York: A Signet Book, New American Library, a division of Penguin Group (USA) Inc. [First published in German in 1957; first published in English in 1958.]

Kaminska, Izabella. 2021. "Do portfolios have a UAP risk?" *Financial Times*, December 10, 2021. https://www.ft.com/content/800e4b4b-d7b0-4fe5-a1ad-2e7f7d4f1ce7.

Karaian, Jason, and Stacy Cowley. 2023. "Regional U.S. Banks Say the Crisis Is Contained, but Fears Persist. *The New York Times*, April 24, 2023, https://www.nytimes.com/2023/04/24/business/regional-banks-crisis.html.

Kaushik, Krishn. 2023. "U.S. tries to woo India away from Russia with display of F-35s, bombers." Reuters, February 17, 2023. https://www.reuters.com/business/aerospace-defense/us-

tries-woo-india-away-russia-with-display-f-35s-
bombers-2023-02-17/.

Kennedy, Charles. 2023. "Saudi Arabia is open to discuss non-
dollar oil trade settlements." *Insider*, January 17, 2023. https://
markets.businessinsider.com/news/stocks/saudi-arabia-is-
open-to-discuss-non-dollar-oil-trade-
settlements-1032023265#:~:text=Saudi%20Arabia%20Is
%20Open%20To%20Discuss%20Non%2DDollar%20Oil
%20Trade%20Settlements,-Start%20Trading%20%3E
%3E&text=Saudi%20Arabia%2C%20the%20world's
%20largest,interview%20in%20Davos%20on%20Tuesday.

KI (Kim Iversen). 2023. "Conversation With Economist Richard
Werner | The Plandemic Was Used To Usher In TOTAL
CONTROL." Originally aired February 24, 2023 on Rumble.
https://www.youtube.com/watch?v=FFAbK20rXa0&t=46s.

Kleveman, Lutz. 2004. *The New Great Game: Blood and Oil in Central
Asia*. Grove Paperback, Grove Press.

Knorr, Wolfgang. 2020. "The age of stability is over, and
coronavirus is just the beginning." The Conversation, April 17,
2020.   https://theconversation.com/the-age-of-stability-is-
over-and-coronavirus-is-just-the-beginning-136380.

LeBor, Adam. 2013. *The Tower of Basel: The Shadowy History of
the Secret Bank that Runs the World*. PublicAffairs, Perseus Books
Group.

LG (Luke Gromen – FFTT, LLC). 2023. "Saudi 'considering'
accepting other currencies for oil, USD weakness, Bank of Japan
brief thoughts." Luke Gromen – FFTT, LLC, January 19, 2023.
https://www.youtube.com/watch?v=I-QopFjnnio.

Losch, Andreas, and Andreas Krebs. 2015. "Implications of the
Discovery of Extraterrestrial Life: A Theological Approach."
Theology and Science 13, no. 2: 230-44. https://
www.tandfonline.com/doi/

full/10.1080/14746700.2015.1023522.

MarketScreener. 2023. "Rothschild: Concordia announces its intention to file a simplified tender offer for the Rothschild & Co shares." MarketScreener, February 6, 2023. https://www.marketscreener.com/quote/stock/ROTHSCHILD-CO-5306/news/Rothschild-Concordia-announces-its-intention-to-file-a-simplified-tender-offer-for-the-Rothschild-42906808/#:~:text=All%20shareholders%20of%20Rothschild%20%26%20Co,registry%20number%20%20499%20208%20932.

Masters, Brooke. 2023. "BlackRock and JPMorgan help set up Ukraine reconstruction bank." *Financial Times*, June 19, 2023. https://www.ft.com/content/3d6041fb-5747-4564-9874-691742aa52a2.

McFate, Sean. 2014., *The Modern Mercenary: Private Armies and What They Mean for World Order*. New York: Oxford University Press.

McGrath, Matt. 2020. "Climate change: US formally withdraws from Paris agreement." *BBC News*, November 4, 2020. https://www.bbc.com/news/science-environment-54797743.

Meessen, A., 2012. "Evidence of Very Strong Low Frequency Magnetic Fields." *PIERS [Progress In Electromagnetics Research Symposium] Proceedings*, Moscow, Russia, August 19-23, 2012. http://www.cobeps.org/pdf/meessen_evidence.pdf.

MEM (Middle East Monitor). 2023. "BRICS discussing decision on Saudi Arabia, Iran memberships this year." *MEM (Middle East Monitor)*, February 16, 2023. https://www.middleeastmonitor.com/20230216-brics-discussing-decision-on-saudi-arabia-iran-memberships-this-year/.

MFARI (Ministry of Foreign Affairs of the Republic of Indonesia). 2023. "Minister of Foreign Affairs Invites BRICS to Fight for

Every Country's Right to Development." Ministry of Foreign Affairs of the Republic of Indonesia. June 3, 2023. https://kemlu.go.id/portal/en/read/4813/berita/minister-of-foreign-affairs-invites-brics-to-fight-for-every-countrys-right-to-development#.

Military.com. 2013. "Report: Israel Passes U.S. Military Technology to China." Military.com, December 24, 2013. https://www.military.com/defensetech/2013/12/24/report-israel-passes-u-s-military-technology-to-china.

Mitra, Anwesha. 2023. "BRICS alliance working to create its own currency, says Russian official." *Mint*, April 2, 2023. https://www.livemint.com/news/world/brics-alliance-working-to-create-its-own-currency-says-russian-official-11680445842563.html.

Navidi, Sandra. 2017. *$uperhubs: How the Financial Elite & Their Networks Rule our World*. Boston, MA: Nicholas Brealey.

NC (The Nuclear Chain). n.d. "Lop Nor, China." The Nuclear Chain. https://www.nuclear-risks.org/en/hibakusha-worldwide/lop-nor.html.

NCTV (New China TV). 2023. "GLOBALink | UN Security Council probe into Nord Stream explosions is global priority: U.S. scholar." *New China TV*, February 23, 2023, https://www.youtube.com/watch?v=1g3UM5VK4qs.

Neutrality Studies. 2023. "NATO Wants Global War | Q&A Nr. 1 With Jeffrey Sachs |Neutrality Studies." Neutrality Studies, June 20, 2023. https://www.youtube.com/watch?v=Y-C9Un-uHD0.

Nicenko, Ana. 2023. "Bank for International Settlements concludes CBDC project 'Icebreakers.'" *Finbold*, March 6, 2023. https://finbold.com/bank-for-international-settlements-concludes-cbdc-project-icebreaker/.

Norton, Ben. 2023. "BRICS challenges US 'dollar dominance',

Saudi considers selling oil in other currencies: New multipolar economic order." *G/E (Geopolitical Economy Report)*, January 21, 2023. https://geopoliticaleconomy.com/2023/01/21/brics-us-dollar-saudi-oil-currency-multipolar/.

NTO (NowThis Originals). 2016. "Central Asia's Post-Soviet Water War Explained." November 15, 2016. https://www.youtube.com/watch?v=vnQeeHwWtFU.

NYT (The New York Times). 1996. "The New Great Game in Asia." *The New York Times*, January 2, 1996. https://www.nytimes.com/1996/01/02/opinion/the-new-great-game-in-asia.html.

Ohlheiser, Abby. 2014. "Pope Francis Says He Would Definitely Baptize Aliens If They Asked Him To." *The Atlantic*, May 12, 2014. https://www.theatlantic.com/international/archive/2014/05/pope-francis-says-he-would-definitely-baptize-aliens-if-they-wanted-it/362106/.

O'Keefe, Eric. 2023. "2022 Land Report: Who Owns the Most Land in the United States?" SuccessfulFarming, January 9, 2023. https://www.agriculture.com/farm-management/farm-land/2022-land-report-who-owns-the-most-land-in-the-united-states.

Oswald, Michael, director. 2014. *Princes of the Yen: Central Banks and the Transformation of the Economy*. Written by Michael Oswald. https:// www.imdb.com/title/tt4172710/. [Also uploaded on Independent POV as "Princes of the Yen | Documentary Film." November 4, 2014. https://www.youtube.com/watch?v=p5Ac7ap_MAY.]

Picken, Andrew, and Stuart Nicolson. 2019. Anders Povlsen: Why a Danish billionaire bought the Highlands. *BBC News*, May 21, 2019. https://www.bbc.com/news/uk-scotland-47803110.

Pope Francis. 2014. "Address of His Holiness Pope Francis on the Occasion of the Inauguration of the Bust in Honour of Pope

Benedict XVI." The Holy See. http://w2.vatican.va/content/francesco/en/speeches/2014/october/documents/papa-francesco_20141027_plenaria-accademia-scienze.html.

Pozsar, Zoltan. 2023. "Great power conflict puts the dollar's exorbitant privilege under threat." Opinion. *Financial Times*, January 20, 2023. https://www.ft.com/content/3e05b491-d781-4865-b0f7-777bc95ebf71.

Prins, Nomi. 2018. *Collusion: How Central Bankers Rigged the World.* New York: Bold Type Books.

———. 2022. *Permanent Distortion: How the Financial Markets Abandoned the Real Economy Forever.* New York: PublicAffairs.

PYMNTS. 2022. "BIS Sets Limits on Bank Exposure to Crypto Markets." PYMNTS, December 18, 2022. https://www.pymnts.com/cryptocurrency/2022/bis-sets-limits-on-bank-exposure-to-crypto-markets/.

Quigley, Carroll. 1966. *Tragedy and Hope: A History of the World in Our Time.* New York: The Macmillan Company.

Randle, Kevin D. 2022. *The Washington Nationals: Flying Saucers over the Capital.* Pontefract, West Yorkshire, U.K.: Flying Disk Press.

Reuters. 2022. "China to use Shanghai exchange for yuan energy deals with Gulf nations – Xi." *Reuters*, December 9, 2022. https://www.reuters.com/business/energy/chinas-xi-tells-gulf-nations-use-shanghai-exchange-yuan-energy-deals-2022-12-09/.

———. 2023. "Riyadh joins Shanghai Cooperation Organization as ties with Beijing grow." *Reuters*, March 29, 2023. https://www.reuters.com/world/riyadh-joins-shanghai-cooperation-organization-ties-with-beijing-grow-2023-03-29/.

Reuters Staff. 2007. "UFO debate invades politicians' space." *Reuters*, December 21, 2007. https://www.reuters.com/article/us-ufo/ufo-debate-invades-politicians-space-idUSN2125757420071221.

Rogan, Tom. 2022. "Unidentified drones sighted flying over US government nuclear labs." *Washington Examiner*, December 22, 2022. https://www.washingtonexaminer.com/opinion/unidentified-drones-sighted-flying-over-us-government-nuclear-labs.

Said, Summer, and Stephen Kalin. 2022. "Saudi Arabia Considers Accepting Yuan Instead of Dollars for Chinese Oil Sales." *The Wall Street Journal*, March 15, 2022. https://www.wsj.com/articles/saudi-arabia-considers-accepting-yuan-instead-of-dollars-for-chinese-oil-sales-11647351541.

Scribner, Cari. 2023. "12 Largest Landowners In The Entire World." Farmland Riches, January 19, 2023. https://www.farmlandriches.com/largest-landowners-world/.

Sguazzin, Antony. 2023. "BRICS Debates Expansion as Iran, Saudi Arabia Seek Entry." *Bloomberg*, February 15, 2023. https://www.bloomberg.com/news/articles/2023-02-15/brics-debates-expansion-as-iran-saudi-arabia-seek-entry?in_source=embedded-checkout-banner.

Smith, Elliot. 2022. "Zelenskyy, BlackRock CEO Fink agree to coordinate Ukraine investment." *CNBC*, December 28, 2022. https://www.cnbc.com/2022/12/28/zelenskyy-blackrock-ceo-fink-agree-to-coordinate-ukraine-investment.html.

SOI (Schmidt Ocean Institute). 2023. "Hydrothermal Hunt At Mariana." Schmidt Ocean Institute. https://schmidtocean.org/cruise/hydrothermal-hunt-at-mariana/.

Stiglitz, Joseph E. 2011. "Of the 1% by the 1%, for the 1%." *Vanity Fair* 53, no. 5 (May 31). https://www.vanityfair.com/

news/2011/05/top-one-percent-201105.

Strauss, Mariana. 2023. "France riots: A legacy of colonial racism? *DW (Deutsche Welle)*, July 3, 2023. https://www.dw.com/en/ frances-colonial-past-and-racism-play-a-role-in-the-uprising- following-nahels-killing-by-police/a-66098959.

Thigpen, Paul. 2022. *Extraterrestrial Intelligence and the Catholic Faith: Are We Alone in the Universe with God and the Angels?* Gastonia, NC: TAN Books.

Totten, Bill. 2003. "Pulling away the curtains from the 'Princes of the Yen.'" *The Japan Times*, August 10, 2003. https://www.japantimes.co.jp/ culture/2003/08/10/books/book-reviews/pulling-away-the- curtains-from-the-princes-of-the-yen/.

UN (United Nations). n.d. Consultative Status with ECOSOC [Economic and Social Council]. https://www.un.org/esa/ coordination/ngo/about.htm.

———. 2002. Treaties and Principles on Outer Space. New York: United Nations. https://www.unoosa.org/pdf/publications/ st_space_11rev2E.pdf.

Vatican Observatory. 2016. "Extraterrestrial Life." Vatican Observatory, September 26, 2016. https:// www.vaticanobservatory.org/education/extraterrestrial-life/.

———. n.d.-b. "Faith Inspiring Science." Vatican Observatory. https://www.vofoundation.org/faith-and-science/.

Webb, Whitney A. 2022. *One Nation Under Blackmail – Vols. 1 and 2: The Sordid Union Between Intelligence and Crime that Gave Rise to Jeffrey Epstein.* Walterville, OR: TrineDay.

Werner, Richard A. 2003. *Princes of the Yen: Central Bankers and the Transformation of the Economy.* London: M.E. Sharpe.

Wikipedia. 2023. "Lawrence Livermore National Laboratory." *Wikipedia: The Free Encyclopedia*, June 15, 2023. https://

en.wikipedia.org/wiki/
Lawrence_Livermore_National_Laboratory.

Wong, Andrea. 2016. "The Untold Story Behind Saudi Arabia's 41-Year U.S. Debt Secret." *Bloomberg*, May 30, 2016. https://www.bloomberg.com/news/features/2016-05-30/the-untold-story-behind-saudi-arabia-s-41-year-u-s-debt-secret?leadSource=uverify%20wall.

WPR (World Population Review). 2022. "Failed States 2022." World Population Review. https://worldpopulationreview.com/country-rankings/failed-states.

Yunita, Shina. 2021. "Mariana Trench: 8 Fascinating Facts About The Earth's Deepest Place." Outside Orbit, April 30, 2021. https://www.orbitinside.com/mariana-trench-fascinating-facts-deepest-place/.

ABOUT THE AUTHOR

Jensine Andresen

Jensine Andresen (Ph.D. Harvard University) holds a B.S.E. in Civil Engineering from Princeton University, where she also earned a Certificate from the School of Public and International Affairs. She completed an M.A. degree at Columbia University in Social Anthropology with a focus on China. She also earned A.M. (master's) and Ph.D. degrees at Harvard University from the Committee on the Study of Religion with a focus on Indo-Tibetan Buddhism.

Dr. Andresen served as a Visiting Assistant Professor at the University of Vermont, where she taught Science and Religion and world religions. She also was an Assistant Professor at Boston University in the interdisciplinary doctoral program on Science, Philosophy, and Religion. Dr. Andresen also held two academic appointments as a Visiting Scholar at Columbia University, and later she was appointed as an Officer of Research, Associate Research Scholar at Columbia. In addition to her work in academia, Dr. Andresen also has held positions in finance, business, and government.